You May Not Be Who You Think You Are!

D1566646

John I. Payne Jr.

NEWMAN SPRINGS PUBLISHING
320 Broad Street
Red Bank, NJ 07701

First originally published by Newman Springs Publishing 2020

ISBN 978-1-64801-584-7 (Paperback)
ISBN 978-1-64801-937-1 (Hardcover)
ISBN 978-1-64801-585-4 (Digital)

Printed in the United States of America

Figure 1. Ada Mae Williams in the 1950s

All that I am and will ever be I owe to my mother, Mrs. Ada Mae (Williams) Hightower. From the moment she first saw me, she loved me. She gave me a strong spiritual foundation, surrounded me with good male role models, and always protected me with her love. Without her discipline, guidance, and unconditional love, I would not be the man I have become. Thank you for loving me!

Your Son,
John Payne, Jr.

For everything that is hidden will eventually be brought into the open, and every secret will be brought to light.

—Mark 4:22 (NLT)

Contents

Foreword

Being adopted can be a challenging experience for everyone involved. As the wife of an adoptee, I have seen, firsthand, the emotional roller coaster of love, fear, abandonment, and insecurities of someone I love. In this book, my husband, John Payne, Jr., writes a compelling, poignant true story about his journey as an adoptee and his search for self.

The book, *You May Not Be Who You Think You Are*, is unique because John takes you on a journey that details his search for self, heritage, and genetic mirroring. The visual representations of John's stories convey emotional attachments and estrangements of family and friends. You will find the discovery of an "Uncle Daddy" and the effects of seeing the resembles of his only daughter in the face of his biological mother. John brings out the emotions of each experience and ultimately demonstrate the vulnerability of most adoptees.

As the wife and forever girlfriend, life partner, and—most importantly—the best friend, I am very proud that John had the courage to tell his story and take the world on his amazing journey of self. This book does not only help adoptees but also helps everyone recognize and embrace the importance of life, vulnerability, self worth, and resiliency. In the end, I am glad John Payne, Jr. chose me to ride along on his journey of self.

Acknowledgments

No one undertakes a journey alone. We depend upon others constantly—in ways both tangible and intangible—to move us toward our destination.
—John C. Maxwell

I would like to thank the following individuals for their research assistance and information sharing. Your knowledge was very instrumental in my efforts to connect with my maternal and paternal bloodlines. I would not have reached the level of success that I was able to achieve—at such a rapid pace—had it not been for your selfless contributions. From the bottom of my heart and with every fiber of my being, thank you Tanya Green, Patricia Hatch, Trevis Hawkins, Laverne Irvin, Francine Jones, Tonya Lynel, and Ronald Smith.

Dr. Rolonda L. Payne, my sweetie, for more than twenty years, your love and support has been unwavering. Thank you for your encouragement, counsel, and the many blessings that come with having you as a life partner.

John I Payne III, Sean Allen Payne, and Jocclyn Makaylah Payne, my dear children, I fought so hard to find my lineage which is also your lineage, and I pray you read about it through the eyes of an adult to gain a fuller understanding of why family is one of the most important institutions on earth. Daddy loves you.

Vanessa L. Williams, you are a steadfast, loving, and an integral part of my life. Your generosity and honesty are fully intertwined with my entire family. I love you for that.

Dr. Eddie L. Harris, Jr., you will forever be my Uncle-Daddy and angel. Your acceptance, love, and wisdom are a beckon of light to me, and your assistance with reintroducing an adopted child to his birth mother is something to acknowledge. Thank you, F.I.E.T.T.S.

Rhonda Rene Ferguson-Lewis, Wednesday, June 20, 2018, will forever be etched into my heart as the most incredible day of my existence. Thank you for being the instrument of God that opened the door to the Ferguson family, healed my soul, and brought peace to my spirit.

Brandon M. Boston, from day one, your friendship has been consistent. You encouraged me in my endeavors and added strength to my belief in the success of "doing!" It is an honor to call you my friend.

Michael Patterson, thank you for your input, opinions, and overall ability to listen. There were so many times when my burden seemed too heavy to carry, but you shouldered some of the weight for me. Also thank you for conducting the first edits of my manuscript. I will forever be in your debt.

Introduction

Born on August 9, 1969, he spent his first seven years, seven months, and twenty-one days without a legal name. The hospital he was born at called him Baby Martin. His impending adoptive parents called him John I. Payne, Jr. It was not until March 30, 1977, when the adoption was finalized that he would forever be known by that name, leaving him to ponder years later: "Who am I and from whom did I come?" Adoption records are sealed and cannot be opened except for non-identifying information such as medical history that may be vital to an adoptee in cases of medical emergency. The adoptive parents are given a copy of the adoption proceedings once finalized. However, years later, adoptees might ask about their biological parents, and some adoptive parents cannot understand why, somehow assuming they haven't done a good enough job at their parental duties.

In some cases, adoptive parents might even hide information from adoptees, not realizing the feeling of guilt about asking in the first place. These are real issues faced by adoptees, and coupled to them is an adoption system that works hard to protect the confidentiality of the adults in the process, giving little provisions for the babies who grow into adults and cannot access vital information needed to heal their souls and provide them with inner peace.

Today, there are numerous ways to identify biological connections including DNA testing, social media, and other procedures. *You May Not Be Who You Think You Are* takes the reader along on John's journey to find his biological mother. It allows the reader to share in his discovery of secrets that arose during his tenacious pilgrimage that also opened doors to genetic mirroring and evidence that he'd seen it earlier in his life without knowing.

On January 19, 1977, John received what he calls, *The Talk*. The woman who raised him or, in simpler words, his mother told him that he was adopted and asked, "If your biological mother wanted you back, would you go?"

He told her, "No, you're my mama!" Years later, he asked his mother for her blessings to find his biological mother, but she refused.

Fifteen years later, she called to say, "I prayed about it and thought it's time for you to find your people."

After years of suppressed feelings of belonging and questions about self, John needed to know more about himself and where he fit in life. During his early years, he thought about having a brother or sister but suspected he was an only child. He also thought about his biological father and mother and wanted to know if they even cared about where he was or who he was becoming. One evening, the walls of his suppressed feelings crashed down on him like a ton of bricks. He needed answers, and he needed them now.

This book is about suppressed feelings and the unsettled peace that comes with not knowing who you are or from whom you came. Readers will feel the pain John experienced when he questioned his lineage, the anguish he experienced during his journey to find his people, and the resulting joy and pain John felt when for the first time he looked at someone else and saw himself.

John began his journey to find the woman who left him at the hospital only three days after he came into existence. His mother, who kept her own secret, provided information that turned out to be the key to untangling the web of deception spun by one woman who long ago decided that John's birth was not meant to be known or seen by others.

Chapter 1

March 1977

On August 9, 1969, at 5:10 a.m., a twenty-two-year-old woman gave birth to a baby at the Orange Memorial Regional Medical Center located in Orlando, Florida. She decided to place the baby into adoption and signed a release of her parental rights to the state of Florida. Three days after giving birth, she left the hospital, and the only thing she left behind was her baby and her name: Mary Alice Martin. I have come to believe in the idea that all children are uncultivated fields of endless possibilities. They can blossom into the efforts invested in them as children by others. These efforts influence their worldviews and equip them for adventures ahead of them in life. Their early development comes from what they see, hear, and are exposed to.

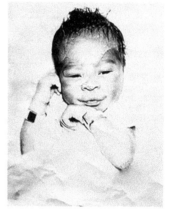

Figure 2. Baby Martin, three days old

Unfortunately, many young men cannot look back to find any positive role models that helped prepare them for what they will encounter in the maze of life. Despite it all, I believe every young man can become a productive human being with morals, values, and integrity, if provided the proper tools. What a man becomes is determined by the efforts—or lack thereof—of parents, guardians, and role models who invested in them. I am of the mind-set, everyone regardless of race, color, or religion inherits some responsibility in the upbringing of our youth. Early on, I realized that I was taught lessons and formed traits, both good and bad from the people around me. Throughout my journey, I have come to many forks in the road, but it was the seeds of good attributes and values planted within me as a child that kept me on the straight and narrow. Those same seeds gave me the courage to turn back when I was heading down the road of self-destruction. Those same attributes have remained a part of my subconscious mind throughout my early years and still serve as the moral compass that guides me today. During my teenage years, I faced many obstacles but managed to escape devastation before disaster struck.

My early years were filled with many lessons provided by my mother and others who entered my life and has left me with a sense of obligation to pass these lessons down to my children, and I hope one day they do the same and pass them on to their children as well. When I was very young, my mother was a devout Baptist, and because of it, spirituality has always played a vital role in my life. Early on, religion was an overwhelming concept for me. In my household, for example, regardless of what cards life may have dealt me during the week, church on Sunday morning was mandatory.

Figure 3. John and Ada Payne in the 1960s

If you wanted to find me on a Sunday morning, you could find me in church! Sunday morning worship taught me dedication which became a value I strongly believe in. As I got older, my mother changed her denomination to Pentecostal or holiness depending on what part of the United States you grew up in. I am not advocating any denomination or religion; however, I personally think having a connection to some form of a faith-based organization can serve as a foundation for strength when times get hard because they will and there is no escaping that. Despite my spiritual upbringing, I was not immune from trouble or the temptations that came along with it. I longed for a father figure or a male role model I could look up to, but my desire alluded me because my adoptive parents were divorced long before my adoption was finalized, and unfortunately, I have no memory of them ever together as a couple. Deep down, I knew that something about our household was different, and I dare to say odd. Most of the kids I knew at the time didn't have fathers in the household as well. My mother kept me involved in church activities, such as the youth choir, youth ushers, and any other programs the church had to offer. In the early years of my childhood, the church seemed to have had tentacles, with a reach that extended well beyond the walls of the church. I couldn't go anywhere without encountering another member of our church, whether at school, the mall, sporting events, and even other neighborhoods.

Without a step-by-step guide to parenting, my mother and other surrogate male role models planted seeds inside me that shaped my views about manhood. The conditions under which I was raised helped develop my core values and instilled within me the ability to dream big.

My mother Ada Mae (Williams) Hightower was born on August 12, 1938, in the small country town of Opelika, Alabama. There, she received her unwavering Christian determination, drive, values, and strong work ethic honed while picking cotton in the smoldering hot summer fields of Alabama. At the age of twenty-one, she left home vowing to move as far away from Alabama as she could. I recall her saying that when she was a child she'd often say, "I'm going to move to the end of the world!"

Ada and John Payne were married by common law after she divorced her first husband and childhood friend, Benny. John was also from Opelika, but they did not know of each other until their paths crossed as young adults after moving to Florida. After a brief courtship, they settled in Apopka, Florida, which is a small Florida town north of the larger metropolitan city of Orlando. Before moving to Florida and marrying John, Ada became pregnant by her hometown husband at the age of eighteen, which was commonplace during the early to mid-1900s. In 1957, during an extremely cold

February winter, Ada gave birth to a premature baby boy at home in Opelika, Alabama.

She placed her newborn baby into a shoebox with a hot water bottle, and along with family, she got into a car and rushed to a hospital in Tuskegee, Alabama, as it was the only hospital closest to her that had an incubator. Ada talked to her baby, prayed, and comforted him as much as she could. The car sped around corners and through the streets; the twenty-eight-mile drive seemed an eternity away, but before she could arrive, her precious baby boy had died. Later, the doctors determined that the cause of death was a case of pneumonia. Ada was devastated by this experience, and her coping mechanisms consisted of anguishing in silence for many years. She longed for the affection and love that only motherhood could offer and expressed her feelings to her husband John and her friend Josephine. Josephine worked as a nurse at the largest hospital in Orlando, Florida, at the time. Since she was a nurse, she saw many cases of adoptions hence why she was able to help Ada feel that powerful affection she was longing for. Soon after sharing her desire with Josephine, a baby was up for adoption; he didn't have a name because the baby's biological mother felt that since she did not desire to raise him, it was not necessary for her to give him a name by which a person is addressed or referred to. Therefore, the state of Florida called him Baby Martin. When John and Ada arrived at the hospital, they could not believe their eyes. They were looking through the glass window of the nursery at a healthy, precious baby boy. In that moment, as soon as they laid eyes on Baby Martin's little face, they both knew he would make a great addition to their family and would fill Ada's long-held desire to have a child she could call her own. They stood there excitedly grinning and smiling and immediately fell in love. The soon-to-be parents talked about how they would come up with the money needed to begin the adoption process. At the time, John was a long-distance truck driver and decided he would donate his travel allowance paid to him by the trucking company for his lodging while on the road. Instead of sleeping in hotels, John made a decision to sleep in the cab of his truck to ensure they had the money to start the adoption process and bring Baby Martin home.

Seven days later and three days after Ada's thirty-first birthday, John and Ada took Baby Martin home. Because of John's sacrifice and their dreams of a well-rounded family, it was easy to settle on an official name for Baby Martin.

Although it would not become legal until March 30, 1977, they agreed Baby Martin would be called John Isham Payne, Jr., named after his adopted father. Their dreams of being a family were short-lived because John battled with alcoholism and frequently became violent while under the influence of his beverage of choice. And because of it, John and Ada were divorced before the adoption of little John was finalized, leaving Ada to became the sole force behind adopting her precious baby boy, John Jr. Following the divorce, she relied upon John Sr. to show up for meetings concerning the adoption and to fulfill his promise to help her become the legal mother of her baby boy. As the years went by, the divorce and the lack of money began to adversely affect the possibility of Ada keeping John Jr.

In 1976, the adoption case was handed over to the Department of Social Services for the purposes of deciding the adequacy of my treatment and environment. As part of the procedures, the court reached out to my biological mother because it needed to determine if she still wanted to relinquish her parental rights. After many attempts to reach her and coming up empty-handed, the court moved forward with the adoption process.

January 19, 1977, was an important day for me, and it also happens to be an historic day in the state of Florida. I recall playing sandlot football with several of my friends in the grass-filled quadrant between the apartment buildings where my mother and I lived. All of us were underdressed for the cold winter temperature, but we had fun laughing and playing anyway. I know this happened a long time ago, and you may not believe me, but it snowed on that day. Yes, it snowed in Florida! I can still remember very vividly opening my mouth to allow the snowflakes to fall onto my tongue; it was amazing! This was also the first time I can remember receiving the talk, not the talk that black parents usually give to their children about staying away from racial dangers or how to act around the police but a different kind of talk. At my mother's request, I walked into the living room and saw her sitting on the couch. She motioned me over to her, and as I stood in front of her, she told me I was adopted. She then revealed some people would be coming by the house later in the week to ask me a few questions.

My mother then asked me, "If your biological mother wanted you back, would you go?" As I observed my mother's face, I could see she was under a great deal of stress. Without hesitation, I replied, "No, you're my momma!" My response was honest and sincere; even at my age, I understood compassion and the power of words. I watched the stress fall away from her face as she extended her arms toward me with open hands and wrapped me tightly in them as tears of joy fell down her face. My mother's feelings were always important to me, and I never wanted to see her hurting or sad. I didn't give much thought to learning that I was adopted nor the people who came by to talk to me. Amazingly enough, it would take me many years to fully understand the gravity and significance of the night when I received the talk. From that day forward, I quickly learned that me and the other children were on two different planets. The talk I was given was much different than the talk my friends received because none of them were adopted like me.

After years of court proceedings, child services interviews, house inspections, and various other evaluations, my adoption was finally finalized on March 16, 1977, although I had been under the care of Ada since my third day on the planet. There were multiple scenarios at play during this period, and being an inquisitive curious child, I needed many things explained to me.

Much of the information I received was provided to me on a level I could understand. The Department of Health and Rehabilitative Services submitted a report on its social investigation about the adoption of John Isham Payne, Jr., involving an interview conducted on December 2, 1976, and filed with the court at 10:01 a.m., December 8, 1976.

The department's report provided recommendations based on the suitability of my adoptive parents, John Isham Payne and Ada Mae Payne. By then, Ada was separated from John, who was forty-one years of age at that time. She entered the relationship in April 1962, and they resided together until June 1971. Ada then married a gentleman by the name of David on September 28, 1973, and said they lived together for approximately six months due to incompatibility. Their marriage was annulled on May 10, 1976. The court found Ada had not legally dissolved her common-law marriage to John.

Cold, Fried Chicken Wings

I can remember it, as if it was yesterday, the day I call "cold, fried chicken wings." The real reason my mother and David divorced will always be one of my greatest lessons on loyalty and unconditional love. I am a product of the 1970s and can only imagine the amount of sacrifice it must have taken for a single mother to raise a child back then.

Before I reached the age of ten, my mother married David, and in the beginning, everything seemingly went well. As long as I can remember, my mother always prepared Sunday dinner, and on this Sunday, she made her famous fried chicken wings. The next afternoon, I returned home from school and immediately rushed to the refrigerator to grab the leftovers; everyone knows Sunday dinners are even better the next day. I was not accustomed to cooking meals at the time, and microwaves were not found in every home, especially ours. Poor people, like us, ate most of our after-school snacks straight from the refrigerator—cold! I peered into the refrigerator, grabbed the plate covered with aluminum foil, and began peeling it away. As soon as the chicken wings were exposed, I grabbed one and began chowing down, licking my fingers in between bites. Another chicken wing quickly disappeared and then another until I had eaten every single piece. I wasn't done! I ran my finger in and around the inside of the aluminum foil to ensure I swiped up the small pieces of golden crust that had fallen from the chicken. When I was satisfied, I placed the plate into the sink and threw the aluminum foil into the trash. Then I sat down to complete my homework, hoping to finish it in time to watch television before bedtime.

David soon walked through the front door and made a beeline to the refrigerator, just like me. Apparently, he thought about

Momma's fried chicken wings all day, just as I had done. He spent a few minutes looking around in the refrigerator, moving things around but not finding what he was looking for. He asked, "Who ate all the chicken?" his voice firm and echoed across the room.

"Me," I said. My gut feeling was telling me to run, and before I knew what was happening, he grabbed me by my arm, removed one of his shoes, and began beating me with it. I began to cry, but I took that beating as much like a man as I could. When David let my arm go, I ran to my room and cried and whimpered. In that moment, I knew when my momma got home, there was going to be a big problem.

I always felt that my mother deserved companionship other than mine. I never wanted to be the cause of turmoil between my mother and her new husband. I decided not to tell her what David had done, but she was always attuned to my feelings. As soon as my mother got home, she realized that I was withholding something. She asked me, "What's the matter?"

I shyly replied, "Nothing."

She changed the tone of her voice and said, "Momma always knows when there's something wrong with her baby. Now tell Momma what's wrong."

I tried with all I could not to tell her, but I couldn't hold back any longer.

I burst into tears and said, "David beat me for eating the left-over chicken."

She said, "What did he beat you with?"

"His shoe," I said.

My momma instantly lost her mind! She had never been a timid woman and did not allow anyone, regardless of their sex, to run over her. If pushed, she could and would fight. That night, I witnessed a one-sided scuffle with my mother in dominate control. During the scuffle, my mother yelled to me, "Go back in your room!" I went back into my bedroom but could still hear her tell David, "You have fifteen minutes to grab whatever you can and leave my house immediately!"

It was on that very evening I learned what loyalty, protection, and unconditional love embodies when physically expressed by someone who cares greatly about you. I never saw David again, and if I walked within inches of him today, I would not recognize him if my life depended on it!

The Final Investigation

By this point, John and Ada did not live together. According to court records, John maintained frequent contact with me during the adoption process. Ada was very active in church and provided me with a spiritual environment throughout.

She gave me a great deal of attention, emotional support, and—most of all, what I needed the most—love. During the investigation, a physician's report on Ada Mae Payne reported normal physical findings. She was unemployed at the time but previously worked as a nurse's aide.

In September 1977, Ada was involved in a minor automobile accident that left her with a neck injury. She received $143.00 in disability payments every two weeks but planned to return to work following doctor's approval. At that time, John had worked for the Fidelity Storage and Transfer Company for nearly twenty years. On average, he earned $135.00 per week. He did not provide Ada with a regular set amount of money but did provide for my needs in the best way he could. My adoption papers show Ada said, John and she contacted the social services director at the Orange Memorial Hospital about adopting a baby in 1969. Approximately one month after their inquiry, they were contacted about my availability. An intermediary placed me in their care when I was released from the hospital.

On August 27, 1969, a petition for adoption was signed by all parties involved and filed with the court in December 1970. On April 21, 1971, this petition was dismissed due to lack of prosecution. Notice of placement was given to the Department of Health and Rehabilitative Services, which was before the 1973 revision to the Adoption Act.

Figure 4. John Payne, Jr. in the second grade, fourth from the left first row.

John had expressed to the court his wishes to be included in the petition as my legal father, which was also Ada's desire. Regarding my suitability as a proper subject for adoption, the birth registration indicated that I was an unnamed male child born on August 9, 1969, to Mary Alice Martin in Orlando, Orange County, Florida. The certificate did not list a father, rather cited an illegitimate birth.

The Department of Health and Rehabilitative Services did not receive any sociological information about the biological mother. They were unable to contact her after consent of an unmarried mother was signed by Alice Martin on August 27, 1969. Thereafter, I was named after my legal father, and from that day, I was known as John Isham Payne, Jr. When I was in the second grade, a physician's report received about me during the investigation stated that I was of reasonable physical condition. According to the adoption records, I had a small physical build and an outgoing and pleasant personality. Observations of me showed that I had a good relationship with my mother and spoke affectionately about my adoptive father. Like many children, I did not understand why my parents were separated.

I was told my adoptive father lived in Apopka, Florida, to be closer to his job. Because John was a long-distance truck driver and usually gone before the separation, this explanation seemed plausible to me, the investigation reported.

Evaluation and Conclusion of the Investigation

According to the birth registration and consent, I was born out of wedlock and placed with John and Ada by an intermediary. Ada provided continuous care from that point, and according to the investigator, it appeared she gave me excellent care and a great deal of love.

Although the prospective adoptive parents were separated after I was placed, the investigator stated John maintained a father-son relationship and the court amended the petition to show the maintenance of the relationship. The biological mother executed a consent for adoption by John Isham Payne and Ada Mae (Williams) Payne.

The Department of Health and Rehabilitative Services

The department recommended the petition for adoption by Ada Mae Payne be granted and recommended adoption by John Isham Payne upon his amendment to the request. While the department did not attempt to take a position on the legalities of the arrangement, it was viewed as being in my best interest.

The department respectfully requested the determination of the court, and the necessary steps were taken to protect the rights of all parties to the proceeding and to assure the legality of my adoption; and with that, my adoption was finalized.

Chapter 2

The Death of a Stranger

A s a child, I felt my father did not love me. As an adult, I am not sure if he did or did not. However, I no longer have a childlike innocence about life and view the world much differently than I did as a child. When I was born, my mother was married to John Payne, and I was placed in their care seven days after my birth, pending finalization of my adoption. Unfortunately, they were divorced before the adoption process was completed. Ada was not discouraged and continued the adoption process as a single parent, which made the process even more difficult than it already was.

Figure 5. John Payne, Sr.
Days in the Military

One of her top priorities was to ensure that I had a positive male role model during my upbringing, which required John to continue to play a role in co-parenting me.

Although I have little to draw from regarding my relationship with him, I spent the bulk of my childhood energy attempting to garner his admiration, love, and respect. In my view, he lacked the desire to give me what I needed to understand the dynamics of a father-son relationship. This lack of passion would have left me without the necessary tools I needed to become the best son, husband, father, and friend if not for the investments made by a few other men whose paths I crossed growing up. Many of the attributes I acquired along the way proved essential, especially when it comes to the kind of relationships I want to build with my wife and children.

My mother shared stories with me about John and her relationship back in the "good old days." None of her stories explained how or why he became an alcoholic, but by the time I was old enough to fully understand, he was totally devoted to alcoholism. I often thought about how alcohol could change a kind and humorous man like him into one of anger and rage.

On his rare occasions of sobriety, he was amusing and pleasant to be around. At other times when filled with his joy juice, he was a totally different person. In my mother's efforts to ensure I received a healthy dose of masculine energy, she would take me to spend time with John on several weekends throughout the year and for one or two weeks during the summer. During these visits, my mother dropped me off at my grandmother's house, and at some point, John would show up to check the box for fatherly obligation. I can only speculate why he continued to entertain me for so many years. Maybe he was making good on his commitment to my mother or perhaps he felt a sense of obligation to assist with the raising of the child they both agreed to adopt.

After serving his enlistment in the U.S. Air Force and several years as a truck driver, John worked as a janitor at the local high school in the town where he lived. Over time, the school system suffered from a janitorial shortage and shifted their human resources to other schools within the school district. This meant John worked closer to where we lived which made our weekend visits more accessible. When John was able to work locally, my mother would take me to his alternate work location. From there, we would travel to the small town where he lived with his mother. Although I knew it would be difficult for me to gain the love of my adoptive father, it didn't stop me from trying. I took advantage of every opportunity, big or small, to garner his attention.

For many years, I have thought about the value John added to our father-son relationship and can identify five memories, ranging from joy to pain.

Little John and the Squirrel

One summer evening, John and I were walking the campus of the well-manicured Bishop Moore High School. At one point, I picked a rock up from the ground and said, "Dad, watch me knock that squirrel out of the tree!"

He quickly replied, "Boy, you can't hit that squirrel!"

Without hesitation and resembling a biblical story, I threw the rock and hit the squirrel. It dropped to the ground, shook off its dizziness, and ran back up the trunk of the tree. John laughed so hard, one of those laughs that originate deep in the chest and involves muscles of the torso. He then extended his arm toward me and patted my head with his right hand with the affection that fathers show their sons. That was a good day!

The Money Game

My mother and I played this game with John to get money for school clothes and an occasional school event. Later in life, I named it the "money game" because you never knew if you were going to win or lose when it came to asking John for money. However, as the years went by, my mother and I got pretty good at the game. To hit our desired mark, we developed a straightforward algorithm to yield what we wanted every time! For example, if we needed fifty dollars, we asked for no less than sixty dollars, and nine times out of ten, he would fall short, thus hitting the mark we set in the first place. There wasn't a single time when John gave more than what we asked for. He was always so predictable.

The Central Florida Fair

The state fair was a big deal to me and thousands of other young Floridians. Every year, we waited with anticipation for the Central Florida Fair. This time was even more special because John vowed to take me to the fair. I was so excited and planned to have the time of my life. Now didn't I mention earlier that John was an alcoholic? When I was a baby, he was a truck driver, but I never saw him behind the wheel of anything. John's sister agreed to drive us to the fair, and on the way, he spotted a liquor store. You guessed it; it was downhill from there!

I can still hear his voice as he enthusiastically said to his sister, "Stop by the All-Boys College!" This was his nickname for a popular liquor store in central Florida in the seventies. John preferred an inexpensive brand of gin and drank it at room temperature straight from the bottle. Once he started drinking, I knew I was in for a very long night!

By the time we reached the fairgrounds, his intoxication had reached its desired level, and he had transformed into everything you would expect of an alcoholic. What was intended to be a great evening of children having fun turned into displays of quick-tempered anger, loud talking, and a bad attitude when I asked to play any game or get on any rides. I spent the entire evening watching my intoxicated, adoptive father playing a variety of the games himself while I struggled to stay clear of his wrath and potential embarrassment in front of others who may have been watching. Somehow, I did manage to make it through that awful disappointing evening.

When I got back to my mother, I couldn't hold back my tears of disappointment any longer. I was so disappointed about making it to the fair but didn't enjoy a single moment while there. My mother scrapped up enough money to take me to the fair on the following weekend. This time was different, and I was able to simply be a kid and enjoy all the fair had to offer.

A Crooked Road

A few months before Ada would remarry, John Payne took a turn at teaching me how to drive a car. In retrospect, I don't think it was wise to have a underaged child behind the wheel of a car while in the passenger seat consuming alcohol as if it was spring water.

However, we did experience a funny and memorable moment, and it would be one of the last happy memories that I have of my adoptive father.

It was a cold winter evening, and we were in an olive drab Ford Mustang that was promised to my cousin by his father when he became of age. While driving my cousin's car with John riding shotgun and my cousin in the back seat laughing at me, they both took turns making fun of my poor driving skills. The car swerved from one side of the road to the other. At one point, John removed a bottle of gin from his coat pocket, took a big swig, and said, "Boy, can't you drive straight?" Before I could respond, he went on to say, "I tell you what, we're going to find you a crooked road. You'll be driving then!"

Although it was at my expense, I was thrilled to see him laugh so hard at my inability to keep the car between the lines without swerving from one side of the road to the other. At the time, I felt his comments were a form of encouragement. As the years passed, I spent less and less time with the man for whom I was named. Other things began to compete for my time such as girls and my love for competitive sports.

Summer Snow

It began with football where my individual skills were above average for my age, then came boxing. I found my way to a police athletic league's boxing team and immediately fell in love with boxing; it was invigorating. For as long as I can remember, I idolized Muhammad Ali. I would do anything to catch his matches on our black-and-white television with the rabbit ear antenna covered with aluminum foil.

One day, while at practice, I sparred with another boxing team member. Boy, did I experience an awakening! At the time, there wasn't anyone on the team in my weight class to spar with, so I was left with a kid in a higher weight class. If I am fortunate enough to live to the age of one hundred, I will never forget the name of the kid who changed the trajectory of my life with a single punch. To save myself the embarrassment, I will *not* reveal his name in this book. We were in the squared circle, and I was showing off my speed and quick foot work. We moved a few steps to the left and then to the right, threw occasional lite jabs, and felt each other out.

Out of nowhere, this kid punched me in the head so hard I saw snow. My head felt like an analog television that lost its signal, and the only thing left visible were random white flickering dots of snow. To avoid getting hit again, I bent over at the waist and stuck my head out of the ropes.

This is the international boxing distress signal for, please don't hit me anymore! The trainer/coach paid me little attention; he was dreaming about the possibility of piling up boxing awards because of the talented pool of boxers on his team who were spread across several weight classes. While my head was still outside of the squared circle, far away from the fist that caused me to place it there, I said a short and silent prayer to God asking, "If you grant me the opportunity to complete this session and get to my bicycle, I would never return, and my boxing career

Figure 6. John Payne, Jr. High School Basketball Sr. Year 1988

would be over!" My trainer/coach was extremely excited because I stood toe-to-toe with someone considered to be the best boxer on our team, and I managed not to get knocked out. The truth was this kid hit me so hard my knees locked up and I couldn't fall, but believe me, I wanted to! Boxing practice ended, and so did my dream of becoming the next Muhammad Ali. I'm sure I walked around for about one week with an untreated concussion. By then, I was convinced that I needed to find a safer sport.

I Was Never There

Basketball proved safer, and I worked extremely hard to become one of the best players in my neighborhood. I thought, if I could measure up to the neighborhood talent, then I could ultimately compete with others elsewhere.

My confidence and skills grew, and I eventually played on both my middle and high school varsity basketball teams. I was never given any special fanfare and didn't expect anyone to attend my games, especially to watch me play.

During a high school game, I looked up into the tiered seating and saw John Payne and one of his coworkers who I remembered from the summers I spent helping my father buff floors. I was completely baffled yet very excited to see my father sitting in the bleachers. When the game was over, I quickly rushed to the locker room to grab my things. I wanted to hurry back to share my excitement about seeing him at my game. When I returned, my father and his coworker were gone, despite witnessing my best basketball playing performance ever. Four years passed before I saw my father again. Although I didn't think about it then, it would be my last opportunity to impress John I. Payne, Sr. I wonder if I was successful?

The One Thing My Father Taught Me

During summer breaks, John Payne allowed me to accompany him to the school where he worked as a janitor. I watched him buff the floor of the long school hallways. On one afternoon, I asked, "Can I buff the floor?" He gave me some quick on-the-job training, and I caught on rather quickly. John then turned the buffer over to me but continued to monitor my work until he felt comfortable about my ability to properly buff the floors without his supervision. When John was comfortable enough, he left me alone to complete the job. I buffed the hallway effortlessly moving the buffer from left to right. It was very important to me to do a good job; one my father would appreciate and be proud of.

Years later, I found myself standing with a group of army privates—mostly strangers to me—being yelled at by a drill sergeant about the condition of our barracks floor. After several minutes of ranting, the drill sergeant grabbed a buffer and cleaning materials and moved them in front of the group. He then said, "I want this floor to be shiny enough for me to see my face in it when I return in the morning!" He then walked out of the barracks leaving everyone standing there, confused and worried about how we were going to accomplish such a insurmountable task. Everyone stood there staring at each other, not saying a word. I looked at the guys for a minute and then took charge.

I divided the privates into teams. Team 1 was responsible for sweeping, team 2 mopping, and team 3 was responsible for spreading the wax. After the teams finished their assignments, I said, "Stay out of my way!" I spent most of the night buffing the hardwood floors to a glass-like shine. The next morning, a different drill sergeant entered the barracks. He stood staring at the floor with a perplexed look on his face, surveying the entire boundaries of the barrack. Then he barked, "Who did this?"

As before, no one responded right away, but then all the guys said in unison while pointing at me, "He did," basically throwing me under the bus!

The drill sergeant looked at me and asked, "Did you do this?"

I responded, "Yes, Drill Sergeant!"

To everyone's surprise, he congratulated me for a job well done. He asked, "Where did you learn how to shine floors like that?"

I replied, "My dad, he's a janitor, and during my summer breaks, he taught me how to buff floors."

The drill sergeant then said, "Well, he taught you well. Good job, Private," while patting me on my back.

My Days in Europe

After completing basic training, my first permanent army assignment was in the Federal Republic of Germany. I was stationed on a small *kaserne*, a German word meaning barracks, called Pond Barracks, located in the German town of Amberg. While in platoon formation, we were asked if we could drive a standard shift vehicle, and to my surprise, I was the only private in the platoon who could operate a standard shift vehicle.

Figure 7. Private John Payne, Jr. in Germany 1990s

As a result, I became the first sergeant's driver and was assigned several military vehicles. A first sergeant is a person who oversees a company (military unit), and most soldiers call him or her "top" because he or she is at the top of the enlisted rank structure within a company. I liked driving all my assigned vehicles, but the two-and-a-half-ton truck that most soldiers called deuce and a half was my favorite.

Many of the Vietnam Veterans still on active duty at the beginning of my enlistment swore they could tell it was me driving a deuce and a half because of the sound they heard from the exhaust pipes.

The deuce and a half made a whistling sound between shifts and a revving of the engine when disengaging the clutch. Germany was a taste of freedom like nothing I had ever imagined. Being in

Germany exposed me to another culture, far different than the one I knew. For me, living and working in Germany was an excellent experience and added so much to my development as a responsible, self-sufficient adult.

In my early twenties, I leased my first apartment in a foreign country, as well as purchased a car on my own. Like most young people with newfound freedom, I partook in the European nightlife quite frequently. One night in 1992, my night did not end as well as the others had. When my night on the town came to an end, I made my way back to Pond Barracks. Shortly after entering my room, I heard a knock at the door and what followed was alarming and unexpected news! I was told, John Payne, the man that I was named after and only father I ever knew, was dying of prostate cancer and could expire at any moment. My transportation was supplied by my unit and was waiting for me outside the barracks.

An airline ticket was purchased by the American Red Cross for my journey home so I could fulfill my father's dying wish to see me in my military uniform. The next morning after arriving home, I put on my uniform and headed to the hospital to see my father.

With no idea of what I was in for, I entered a two-patient hospital room to a man that was all but recognizable. John Payne suffered from prostate cancer, and his refusal to accept medication and treatment, due to his lack of will to live, caused me to nearly walk past him to check the other bed furthest from the door to look for someone that resembled the man I traveled so far to see. As I walked toward the foot of the next bed, he called out to me with a great deal of enthusiasm, "Hey, boy!" We talked for a while, and he explained to me he had accepted his fate and no longer wanted to fight what he believed to be a lost cause.

I pleaded with him to not give up so quickly, and eventually, he surrendered to my pleadings and agreed to fight for whatever life he had left.

Subsequently, our heartfelt, one-on-one, man-to-man conversation paid off, and I requested to speak with his doctor to explain his change of heart. From that day forward, he was very receptive to medication and treatment, and after a few months, he showed significant progress. My father gained his weight back and looked like his old self again.

His progress showed so much improvement he was released from the hospital as an outpatient. Following his release, I requested return to Germany, and two weeks after returning, I decided to enjoy the nightlife again as I had done in the past. Like déjà vu, after returning from a night in the streets, I heard a knock at my door. I was given the troubling and unfortunate news that my father had passed away.

I returned home to attend my father's funeral; however, it turned into the burden of burying a man who had not taken any steps to get his affairs in order. I was left with the responsibility for making his funeral arrangements and paying for it too. Strangely enough, I can't recall much about the funeral service. However, there are a few details that have lingered in my mind for years. My father had a group of friends he worked with, and I remember each of them filing into the church to pay their final respects to their friend and coworker. I can recall how I felt when I saw them after so many years. I thought about the many summers I spent with them and how much they had aged over the years. Because my father was a veteran of the armed forces, I was able to get him a headstone. I later thought, how strange it was for me to see a headstone with my name on it.

Although my father couldn't provide me with the level of attention I needed and wanted, he did fulfill his promise to his ex-wife and friend by serving as a male role model to me, his adopted son.

By keeping his promise, it brought some form of balance to my life and provided me with both a maternal and paternal structure that I could call my own. I never received the chance to really know my adoptive father nor did I get an opportunity to thank him for his contributions to my upbringing. So I will do it now.

> Thank you, John Isham Payne, Sr., for keeping your promise to the best of your ability. Today, I no longer view the world as a child. I now realize the effort, discipline, and sacrifice it must have taken for you to allow an ex-wife and an adopted child to periodically impose interrup-

tions on your life for eighteen years. As a husband of twenty years and father of three children of my own, I can only imagine the complexities of co-parenting an adopted child with a woman whom you no longer were involved. Thank you, Dad, for allowing me to partake in the cohesive love and fellowship of the Payne and Freeman families, I am eternally grateful!

Your Son,
John Isham Payne, Jr.

Chapter 3

Acquiring Manhood

As a young boy, one of my mother's priorities was for me to have a male role model in my life to provide me with the foundations of manhood. There are a few men that crossed my path like perfect storms. Seemingly, they appeared at just the right intervals to provide me with what I call man skills. Man skills are the hard and soft skills a young boy receives from his father, male role models, mentors, or even big brothers. Many of these attributes shape the beliefs and values he carries with him for a lifetime. It is challenging for me to pinpoint one person, reason, or situation that explains why I am the way I am or defines who I have become. Therefore, I choose to acknowledge the contributions of a diverse group of men, each different than the other.

Henry Prime

As a youth, it literally felt as if I spent my life in church every day of the week and all day on Sundays. Seriously, Sunday mornings began with Sunday school, seamlessly morphed into Sunday morning worship service, and then migrated into the church cafeteria for Sunday dinner the mothers of the church prepared. Just when I thought it was over, the evening worship service began, and it could literally last well into the night. When I say literally, I mean literally!

In the 1970s, my mother was Baptist, and because I was a child, her religion was automatically my religion. Back then, the church members in the black community banded together to help one another with just about anything. There was always someone willing to stand in the gap to assist a fellow church member in need. Henry Prime was an older gentleman and a deacon at the church. He took an interest in me and became my best friend and mentor. Henry didn't have a car; he caught the bus or walked all around the city. To pick up extra cash, Deacon Prime cleaned the church and maintained the grounds. I found myself spending lots of time with him. He took me under his wings, and believe it or not, he subcontracted his work at the church out to me. This allowed me to pick up some much-needed change to purchase small items that little boys desired.

Figure 8. Henry Prime in the 1970s

Although I did not understand what Henry was doing at the time, he taught me life skills and the value of hard work. For example, I can vividly recall him teaching me how to clean a toilet, use a vacuum, properly sweep and mop floors, and how to rake leaves and cut grass.

Figure 9. Senior living high rise building in Orlando, Florida

Early Saturday mornings, Henry and I would clean the church, inside and out, and then he paid me for the work I did from his pay. He would also hold back a portion of my pay as savings. Henry always said, "It's important to save some money for a rainy day!" which never made sense to me as a kid; now as an adult, I get it. Henry lived in the Lake Lorna Doone Senior Citizens Building, which was within walking distance of the church. Sometimes, my mother allowed me to spend the night with him and return home after church on Sunday.

When I was with him, he never wasted an opportunity to teach me a lesson, and I have passed many of those lessons to my sons at one point or another. Henry was instrumental in molding my perceptions of what a man is supposed to be and the things a man should know to take care of himself. He taught me the proper way to dress, how to take care of my belongings, how to iron my clothes, shine my shoes, tie a tie, and even the importance of a haircut. Sometimes, Henry allowed me to cook dinner for us, and then we sat around talking about everything under the sun. He was an incredible example of manhood, and the lessons he taught me would lay dormant deep within me until I made my transition into manhood.

Years after he died, I found myself reflecting on our times together and the wisdom-based thoughts of common sense that he shared with me. They have become an essential part of who I am today. I can recall the time I needed a bed to sleep on. When our work was done at the church, Henry and I walked across town to the furniture store. Once inside, he helped me select a bed and then said, "We're going to use your rainy-day money to buy your very own bed." I was extremely surprised and walked out of the furniture store with a sense of personal pride that has been difficult to match. I held my head high, stuck my chest out, and believed that through hard work, I earned something that made my life just a little better. Looking back through the eyes of a man, I realize that I did not earn enough money to buy that bed. Henry was planting the seeds of dignity, determination, drive, and a desire for self-sufficient sustainability in me. Our time together became less frequent, but the lessons Henry taught me became even more valuable as I transitioned more and more into manhood.

My best friend and mentor grew older, and his family eventually moved him back to his hometown of Jacksonville, Florida, so they could more easily oversee his care. Within a few years after I joined the army, Henry passed away. His passing is still extremely painful for me. At the time of his passing, the army wouldn't allow me to return home to pay my respects to my dear friend and mentor.

The only regrets I have from my childhood is that I never got the opportunity to tell Henry thank you and to pay my final respects to my friend.

"Thank you, my dear friend, for your wisdom and for seeing something in me that allowed you to bestow a fraction of your wisdom upon me!"

Pop's Teachings

On August 28, 1979, my mother married my stepfather, John Hightower, Jr., who I affectionately call Pop. As a young boy, Pop taught me several skills that I feel every man should know. For example, when I began to show an interest in cars, he decided to provide me with hands-on training that began with verbal instructions on the tools needed to change a tire. After helping me to form a mental picture, he took me out onto the driveway and began instructing me in the steps needed to change a tire on his truck as if the tire was flat. Pop's style of teaching was slow, deliberate, and methodical.

*Figure 10. John Hightower (Pop) and John Payne III
fishing on Lake Sunset Orlando, Florida*

He always wanted to ensure that I comprehended every single step in each process. Not only did he teach me how to change a tire, but also he taught me how to change the oil and breaks using his truck for hands-on training. Pop took me fishing too, and during those excursions, he taught me how to bait a fishing hook and how to care for my fishing tackle.

Pop also has multiple admiral attributes such as the patience of Job, strength of Samson, faithfulness of King David, and the wisdom of Solomon. When the time came for me to teach my oldest son how to bait a hook, I learned firsthand how much patience Pop must have had to get me to trust him enough to reach my hand into a Styrofoam cup and grab a live earthworm. To my credit, my son learned how to bait a fishing hook at an early age too. However, I didn't show him the same level of patience Pop showed me when teaching me how to bait a hook, I didn't have Pop's capacity for patience. I found myself having to step aside to allow my son to be schooled by Pop's slow and methodical teaching style, and the many things about life that Pop shared with me when I was a young boy. To date, my oldest son and I still love to go fishing.

Bernard and Ms. Helena

Pop had several nephews who became surrogate big brothers to me. I had the pleasure of learning something from each of them, and those experiences played a major role in my foundation of manhood. Bernard had completed a four-year enlistment in the U.S. Army and asked my parents if he could live with us for a short period while he transitioned back into civilian life. From my perspective, he represented the smooth-talking player. Bernard was the first black man I met who appeared to have it all together.

He was young, clean cut, and fit. His name-brand clothes seemed tailored made just for him, and his matching custom-painted car, truck, and motorcycle added to his image. Although he was my cousin, by way of my mother's marriage to his uncle, he was old enough to be my uncle. Bernard's brief presence in my life taught me how to be confident.

When I was a young boy, there was a woman who lived in the neighborhood name Ms. Helena. She was known for providing everyone in the neighborhood something to gossip about. Some neighbors spoke highly of her, mostly men and young boys. Other neighbors spoke badly about her because of the sexy attire she wore and/or her profession, which they viewed as unacceptable for a lady. The truth is, Ms. Helena was an ebony goddess and the object of desire for every man and boy in the neighborhood. When she walked up and down the street, every man, woman, and child paid attention. Even I committed the sin of lust several times while watching her.

One afternoon while playing football in the street with friends, I saw Bernard standing on Ms. Helena's front porch. Most of the men in the neighborhood desired Ms. Helena, but none would openly approach her because of the scrutiny they may have faced from other people in the neighborhood, but it didn't stop Bernard. There he was, openly making his move on Ms. Helena. My friends and I continued to play football but were only pretending to do so. We moved closer and closer to the action. Our intent was to eavesdrop on their conversation. My friends and I took turns throwing the football toward where they were standing so we could be near the action.

As the sun started to set and the streetlights began to flicker signaling it was time for me to go in the house, I was then called into the house to shower and eat dinner. After eating dinner, I sat down to watch television until bedtime. I sat there hoping Bernard walked through the door, but he didn't come home that night.

During the early hours on the next morning, Bernard quietly slipped into the house without detection by my parents, but I awoke to find him sitting beside my bed with a big smile on his face. He shared a few hot details with me about his triumphant night with Ms. Helena. Looking back, I was far too young to hear the intricate details of his X-rated experience, but I was happy that his confidence and persistence paid off.

I looked up to Bernard, he was my first example for having courage when you interact with the opposite sex. On dating, he was fearless, regardless of a woman's physical attributes or social status. Bernard taught me that confidence is a premium attribute that I would need when it came time for me to date. Bernard eventually moved away, and another one of Pop's nephews seamlessly took his spot at our house.

John "Cheese" Wilson

Anyone that knows John Wilson well calls him Cheese because he always smiled as if he was about to take a picture. I was fifty years old before I learned his full, real name. At the time, Cheese was the closest thing to what a big brother would have been to me. He always called me Tyke, and I believe it was his form of endearment. I wore his nickname like a badge of honor because Cheese was the only person who called me by that name. He dedicated a great deal of his time to me, and he was very instrumental in guiding me through my early adolescent years.

Figure 11. John "Cheese" Wilson

Cheese took over where Henry left off including teaching me life lessons that I will forever be grateful. Both of us loved basketball, and he used it to establish rapport with me and to gain my trust. We would talk for hours and hours at basketball courts around the city. Cheese entered my life at the time I was becoming interested in girls. Looking back, maybe Ms. Helena was the first to peak my interest about girls. I am more than sure that by this time I had already committed the sin of lust while watching her. Cheese was more than a big brother to me; he was my guardian angel and set the standard for being a gentleman and how to treat a woman. Cheese arranged and chaperoned my first few dates and talked to the parents of girls I was interested in to discuss my good character and qualities before the parents even met me.

He taught me how to drive a car even though I couldn't master the manual shift in his Subaru coupe. In first gear, I usually choked. A tricky thing about driving manual cars is you have to press down the clutch and the accelerator at the same time until you get to the point where the transmission is engaged and then slowly release the clutch to press more on the accelerator. It's probably easier said than done, but once you get used to it, it's like riding a bike. Nowadays, many people drive automatic cars, but only people who are really passionate about cars know that you can't call yourself a driver until you learn to drive manual.

One Saturday afternoon following several hours of basketball at the park, Cheese drove me to the other side of town for pizza. After arriving, Cheese sat quietly listening to my concerns about church, girls, school, and my parents. After we filled up on pizza, we returned to the car where we sat with the windows rolled down enjoying the great Florida weather and talking about a wide range of issues. Suddenly, a city bus pulled up to a nearby bus stop. Cheese quickly exited the car and began walking toward the bus stop. He looked back and forth between the bus and me and at one point said, "See you when you get home!" Cheese got on the bus, paid his fare, sat down, and the bus drove away. I couldn't believe he left me!

I sat there in the passenger seat, startled and wondering what to do. I thought, *How am I going to get home?* Once I gained enough courage, I slid into the driver's seat and adjusted myself behind the steering wheel, started the engine, placed the shift in reverse, then first gear, and slowly drove away. At the tender age of thirteen, I was years away from a driver's permit and even further from driver's license, but I drove several miles across town without breaking a single traffic violation. I was filled with pride as I drove down the street where I played football as a child and watched Ms. Helena walk up and down the sidewalk. When I arrived home, every man who meant something to me at that time was there waiting for me.

Pop, Bernard, and Cheese moved to the edges of the driveway as if to avoid being run over. I slowly but efficiently pulled into the driveway. There had never been a day before when I felt such gratitude.

Pop just smiled, Bernard spoke to me as if seeing me drive was an everyday occurrence, and Cheese said, "I knew you could do it, Tyke. I had faith in you man!"

After that day, Cheese began to trust me with his car and allowed me to drive alone every now and then. My confidence grew exponentially during the years Cheese spent listening to me and sharing his wisdom with me, but all good things come to an end.

I became a little older, moved on to middle school, and then to high school. Eventually, Cheese and his then girlfriend were married, and he became the father of three beautiful and successful daughters.

Fools Valley

Growing up, my mother often spoke about a place called Fools Valley. I always listened to her, but I couldn't figure out if she was talking about a real place or using a metaphor to describe certain behaviors or negative events. As I grew older, I came to the realization that Fools Valley wasn't a physical location. It's a state of mind or self-created troubling path that many of us find ourselves on as we journey into adulthood.

When I began writing this book, my aim was to present myself in the best possible light. However, a very close friend of mind told me that I couldn't tell my story without being totally open and honest about all my experiences. After deep thought and overwhelming fear about being totally open about my experiences, I came to realize that it is imperative that I tell it all, including my journey into the depths of Fools Valley.

One evening during my senior year in high school, I was driving with a car full of my closest friends. We were headed to an out-of-town high school football game. After picking up my last passenger, we began what turned out to be a two-hour drive. After a few miles,

I turned onto the entrance ramp of a toll road which was the fastest route to our destination. When I pulled up to the toll booth, I completely stopped the car to throw my quarters into the collection basket. I sat with my foot on the break waiting for the light to turn green, but it seemed to be taking an excessive amount of time to change. I glanced into the basket and simultaneously heard the faint sound of a ringing alarm. I thought, most likely because of the long time it was taking for the light

Figure 12. A toll collection basket

to turn green. I took a second look into the collection basket to see if my quarters were accepted and couldn't believe my eyes. The collection basket was filled with quarters. Without any hesitation, my friends and I immediately jumped out of the car and began stuffing quarters into our pockets. When we ran out of pocket space, we began to shovel the remainder of the quarters directly into the car with our hands until the collection basket was nearly empty. Before I got back into the car, I noticed that someone had placed a wad of aluminum foil at the bottom of the collection basket which prevented the quarters from falling through the bottom of the collection basket to be tallied. I thought, maybe some homeless person placed the foil in the collection basket and had not made it back to complete their plan before we came along and spoiled it. To us, it was a blessing from heaven, a gift, and a great opportunity for anyone who needed some money.

When we arrived at the game, we paid our admission in quarters. We even shared our trifling acquired wealth with other classmates at the concession stand during halftime. After the game, we continued to flaunt our newfound wealth with our friends at the local Burger King before we decided to head home. We financed our entire night of festivities with the quarters and blew most of our unearned money just as quickly as we had jumped out of the car to grab it. When we returned to Orlando, I dropped all my friends at home except for one because I had decided to spend the night at his house. I recall having mixed emotions about what we had done, but the peer pressure was much too strong for me. At the time, I couldn't resist the temptation of readily available money and wanting to be accepted by the crew. However, I cannot help but admit that night was one of the most fun I ever had as a teenager.

For several days after our quarter-filled weekend, I moved around the city with my senses on high alert. It felt as if I was a fugitive from justice living on borrowed time and law enforcement was coming to arrest me at any moment, but they never did. At the end of each lesson taught, a test usually follows, and life is no different. Toward the end of my senior year in high school, life began to throw a series of curveballs at me. Each situation tested my resolve and the tensile strength of the attributes and values I had been given up to that point in life. A friend and I began to discuss different ways we could make some money and decided that we would sell drugs. I knew what we decided was wrong, but the influence of money and our friendship clouded my judgment. So I moved forward with our plan. We combined our limited funds to serve as the initial investment into our new business and bought our first eight ball of crack cocaine.

My friend schooled me in the underworld of crack dealing. He acquired his knowledge and skills from his stepfather who dabbled in the drug and pimp game from time to time to make ends meet. We bought everything we needed to support our illegal business activity from the local Korean corner store. I couldn't help but think why such items were sold in a corner store, and after so many years of visiting the store I had not noticed them. I asked myself, "Why would anyone need miniature ziplock bags? How is selling this stuff legal?" After becoming more aware of my surroundings, I came to understand that miniature sandwich bags are sold across the city only in neighborhoods like mine. This bothered me back then, and it still does today! On the next day after our initial purchase, we set up shop at a local basketball court that was tucked away on the other side of a bridge that ran over a man-made canal and extended out to a lake. Within a few hours, we turned our $75.00 investment into $350.00 and bought more crack on that very day. Although young, misguided entrepreneurs, my friend and business partner had a fierce reputation, which made the likelihood of us being taken advantage of very unlikely. So the natural order of progression was to expand, and within a matter of weeks, we began hiring other neighborhood kids to do our dirty work.

Their job was to make sales on the street corner for a small percentage of the total profit made from the drugs we supplied each of them. During one of my evening drop-offs and pickups to a street corner guy at his grandmother's home where he lived. His grandmother pulled me to the side and whispered, "A friend of mine gave me some money and want to purchase some crack." I sold her two rocks for twenty dollars.

A week later, I was running my route and ran into the same grandmother. At one point while standing together, she said, "Look, baby, I don't have no money, but ah, can I buy some crack on credit until I get my check on the first of the month?" Instantly, it dawned on me that the sales were not for her friend but for her. Coming to this realization hit me hard, felt surreal, and nearly brought me to tears. As I drove off, I began to reflect on my life and thought about how far I had strayed away from the values I was taught by Henry, Pop, Bernard, Cheese, and—most importantly—my mother. I suddenly said to myself, "You've traveled deep into Fools Valley!" I began thinking about avenues I could take to better my life and immediately started formulating plans. I imagined having children and providing them with a loving and stable home environment. It was if my whole life was flashing before my eyes.

I dreamed of attending college, but at the time, I felt my days of substandard academia had taken its toll on me, and furthering my education seemed the equivalent to climbing Mount Everest.

Growing up in the environment that I did, it was imperative that you developed and maintained a high level of mental toughness, but I possessed something that most children around me did not have—a conscience. As an early youth, I was molded into a young man with deep spiritual ties that always diverted me back onto the straight and narrow path. I can still hear my mother praying for me, asking God to shield me from all hurt, harm, and danger, to crown my head with wisdom and knowledge.

After examining my actions, thoughts, and feelings, I decided to join the military for a few years. I hoped it would give me the opportunity to grow and somehow allow me to earn a college degree. What struck me the hardest was the thought of everyone who wanted to be someone was already out in the world becoming somebody! I realized that I needed to strike out on a positive journey that would yield a return on my mother's investment. After enlisting in the U.S. Army, I couldn't immediately leave Orlando. I had to wait for two weeks before I could depart for basic training. Two weeks wasn't a long time, but the wait felt like an eternity to me.

During the last two weeks at home, I avoided my friends and members of the old crowd. I made myself hard to find in fear of getting into trouble or losing my opportunity to change the current trajectory of my life.

The Purge

One afternoon while waiting to depart for basic training, I drove to Checker Park where I knew people liked to hang out. After coming to a stop, I got out, walked to the trunk and opened it, and began handing out my gold chains and other jewelry, clothes, and the ill-gained money I had on me.

Some of the people receiving my goods asked, "What's up with you man?"

Others simply said, "Aw, man, thank you!"

As I handed the items and money away, I felt a sense of shedding the old for the new. In my very soul, I was determined to change my life. When everything was gone, I said, "Hey, you guys enjoy yourselves, I'm gone." I walked to my car, got inside, and drove straight home.

Once it was time for me to depart my hometown, my mother drove me to the recruiters' office, and on the way, we talked about the experiences I may have by joining the army; at other times, we sat quietly, experiencing our own personal reflections. When we arrived, we exited the car to say goodbye. My mother hugged me with teary eyes and said, "Goodbye, baby. Momma loves you. You be good!"

With a pain in my chest and tears building up in my eye, I said, "Awe, Momma, I love you! You know I'll be good!" and then walked toward a van waiting to transport me and other enlistees to the Tampa, Florida, Military Entrance Processing Station (MEPS). I climbed into the van and looked around at the other guys onboard. I found a seat next to a window and looked out at my mother, still standing there heavyheartly smiling at me and waving goodbye. I waved back as tears began to well in my eyes. I looked around the van to see if anyone could see me crying and noticed that some of them were crying too.

They were also experiencing the pain of leaving loved ones behind while also feeling insecure about what lie ahead. The van pulled away, and I continued to look out the window at my mother until I could no longer see her. For several miles, everyone sat quietly, the air was filled with fear and excitement at the same time. We eventually began to cautiously interact with each other. We were scared of the unknown, but the new life ahead made us hopeful of a better life. We talked about our reasons for joining the military and rambled about the unknown.

Garrett DeBose

Garrett was one of the guys I met in the van on my way to basic training. Through conversation, we learned that we graduated from the same high school, which I found to be very comforting because I no longer felt I would travel this road alone. We talked about our years in high school, locations around the city, and what we shared in common.

Figure 13. Pvt. DeBose in Amberg, Germany 1990s

By the time we arrived at the MEPS, we had formed a bond that I am sure will last a lifetime. Garrett and I completed Basic Training and Advanced Individual Training (AIT) together. After AIT, we were sent to Germany and assigned to the same unit and platoon despite being told several times we would more than likely be sent to different locations.

Shortly after arriving to our unit in Europe, I was involved in a physical altercation with another private. I have never figured out the reason, but we were at odds at first sight. We were very competitive toward each other and continuously went back and forth about everything. We were like two gamecock roosters placed on the same farm, the roosters with the highest levels of testosterone would rule, so naturally one day, it all blew up. At that moment, I was feeling rather bold because I had my big brother standing in my corner. Garrett didn't hesitate to let the others know that the fight would be fair and that I was more than capable of holding my own, but I knew that if I needed help, he would be in the ready to jump in if I needed him to.

He always kept a watchful eye on me but never intervened, unless it was absolutely necessary.

Garrett played a vital role in my life and helped propel me further into manhood. In my heart, he will always be my first big brother! No matter what I did, he has always had my back. His unwavering encouragement, brotherly love, and support provided me with the courage and motivation to believe in myself. Time moved on, and the army finally split us up, but we've stayed in touch over the years. Like a real big brother, Garrett has always been sincerely proud of my accomplishments.

When we're together, we still laugh and reminisce about the good old days when both of us were young army privates serving our country halfway around the world, away from home for the first time in our lives.

Johnny "Sniper" Graham

In 1993, while stationed in the Federal Republic of Korea, I met a fellow sergeant name Johnny Graham. The name, Sniper, was given to him by a mutual friend, and the use of that name is reserved for those of us who served together in Korea. During our years stationed together, we developed a lifelong friendship that has lasted for over twenty years. Our friendship has survived the changes we both have gone through.

Figure 14. MSG Johnny (Sniper) Graham

Growing and becoming more mature each day, we have managed to grow up together and not grow apart over the years. In 2007, on a cold Maryland winter morning, I received an unexpected call from Johnny while at work. I always enjoyed Sniper's calls because he lived such an exciting military life, most of which he couldn't discuss due to the confidential nature of his assignments after he left Korea.

I always compared his military career to the hit television show, *The Unit*. At some point during our conversation, I asked, "Where are you currently located?"

He said, "Man, I can't tell you where I am, but I will call you back in a few hours to let you know where I am later today." A few hours passed, and Sniper called me back. He told me he was on a security detail in a Middle Eastern country.

I then asked, "Man, where are you now?"

Like many of our conversations, he said, "I am not at liberty to provide you with an answer to your question." Later that evening, Sniper called me again to confirm my address. He wanted to ensure he was parked in the correct driveway. After miles of travel over several foreign countries and attending a meeting at the Pentagon, Sniper stopped by to spend a little time with his army buddy before traveling home to his family in South Carolina. My dear friend Johnny is always full of surprises!

In 2008, I decided to retire from the army after twenty years of honorable service. Back then, Johnny was stationed at MacDill

Air Force Base located in Tampa, Florida. He deemed my retirement ceremony important enough to drive from Tampa, Florida, to Baltimore, Maryland. During the after-party, Sniper and I had a private conversation, and he said, "John, seeing you retire helped me decide that it's time for me to retire too."

At that moment, I said, "I'll be in attendance whenever you decide to retire!" The earnest friendship of others is very special to me, and I reciprocate my earnest friendship through my actions.

If I give my word, I see it through at all costs. When Sniper retired, I traveled to Tampa, Florida, to repay my friend for his unwavering friendship, his service to our country, and to his family for supporting him throughout the years. Now that we're older, I've found myself reminiscing about his daughter babysitting my children on several occasions. We've come a long way from our days in Korea, my dear and honorable friend.

Fordham and My Professional Development

Throughout my life, God has sent several guardian angels in human form to guide and watch over me when danger was lurking in the shadows. My tour in Korea turned out to be a pivotal moment in my military career and personal life as well. My resolve was tested during my fifty-two-week Korean tour of duty, and without fail, God sent me another guardian angel to walk with me and keep me company through the journey that was ahead of me. As I approached the end of my tour, I was asked if I wanted to appear before a promotion board. I quickly responded, "Most definitely," and I immediately began the rigorous study to prepare for what I knew would be a challenging hurdle.

For me, advancement to the next higher rank would place me ahead of the average promotion pace of my peers. On the day of the board, I was meticulous in my preparations because I didn't want to leave anything to chance. When I walked into the building at battalion headquarters, I felt so nervous that it seemed I was about to vomit all over my uniform, awards, and decorations. I sat down on a bench next to older, more seasoned sergeants and watched each of them enter the conference room where the board was being conducted. As they exited, each had a look of defeat on their faces. It was as if they had fallen short of a lifetime opportunity. There I was, sitting alone at the end of the bench waiting to be called. On that day, I needed to express courtesy and every military custom that I knew to be successful before the board. I was instructed to approach the door of the conference room and knock, and after knocking, I would hear a voice granting me permission to enter.

When called, I stood at the door and knocked so hard one would have assumed it was the police, ready to make an arrest. I heard a voice of authority say, "Enter!" I entered the room, taking extra precautions to execute my facing movements with accuracy and precision. I walked over to a chair situated in the middle of the room and centered on the front of the table where the board members were seated. Once seated, my shoulders were erect, feet placed at shoulder width apart, and my arms were extended with the palms of my hands resting on my knees. What happened during the board is a blur, but in the end, a voice of authority said, "Dismissed!" I got up from the chair and stood at the position of attention. I then left the conference room executing the same level of accurate and precise facing movement I used to enter the room. I sat on the bench outside the conference room, waiting like an expectant father.

Figure 15. SFC Bernard Fordham

After a few minutes, my supervisor exited the conference room to inform me of the results, and he did not hesitate to say, "Although you answered every question correctly and didn't have any uniform deficiencies, you didn't pass the promotion board." He seemed elated to provide me with his opinion about why I failed. Apparently, my age was a problem for the board. They believed I was simply too young to be promoted to the next higher rank. While in Korea, I dedicated myself to becoming the best possible soldier I was capable of becoming. I volunteered for multiple additional duties to occupy my time. I thought that if I immersed myself in multiple activities, my time in Korea would quickly pass, and before I knew it, I would be on my way back to the United States.

After receiving my clearing papers, I needed my commander's signature before I could depart. When I met with my commander to obtain his signature, he asked, "Are you promotable?"

I said, "No, sir! I recently attended a promotion board and answered all the questions correctly, but the board felt my age was a problem." Later, I found out that the board didn't have a problem, it was my supervisor who felt I was too young and advancing too quickly.

My commander ordered me to, "Find your supervisor and have him report to me immediately!"

I left the commander's office to locate my supervisor. Once found, I told him, "The commander wants to see you right now!" I accompanied him to the commander's office. We both entered his office, and I watched in amazement as the commander reprimanded my supervisor for his actions during my promotion board. After the commander was done, he called the personnel human resources office to speak with Sergeant First Class Fordham. Because I was due to depart Korea in two days, my commander placed everyone on notice that no one could be released from work until paperwork was completed that would allow me to appear before a promotion board on the very next day. I thanked my commander for his faith in me and for giving me an opportunity for growth and professional development. I also expressed discomfort with the prospect of my supervisor sponsoring me before the board for a second time. My commander then authorized me to identify any noncommissioned officer under his command of my choosing to act as my sponsor. On the next morning, I reported to the conference room for a second time, but this time felt different. My confidence level was higher than before because I knew what to expect from the board members.

When I entered the conference room, I was shocked to see my supervisor sitting at the table, alongside the other panel members. Instantly, a fleeting but not so good thought ran across my mind.

In that moment, I refused to give him the satisfaction of being a witness to any display of nervousness just because he was present. Like before, I answered every single question correctly that the panel members could throw at me. One panel member remained, my supervisor, who drilled me much more stringently than the others, and I will never forget what happened next. He looked me directly in my eyes and said, "Sergeant Payne, your next question has two parts, and I expect two answers!"

"Who wrote the lyrics, and who composed the music to our national anthem?" After he was done, I saw a smirk on his face and thought about the joy he felt in

Figure 16. Bernard and John at John's fiftieth birthday party

his belief that he won, proving his point that I was not suitable for advancement at that time.

I sat quietly for a moment and then looked away from the panel, pretending to be searching deep inside myself for the answers. I thought, *Wow, he wants to trip me up so bad.* After toying with him for a few more seconds, I looked directly into his eyes and answered, "Francis Scott Key wrote the lyrics, and John Stafford composed the music."

Immediately after providing my answers, the president of the panel barked, "I have heard enough. Sergeant Payne, you are dismissed!" I stood, rendered a salute, and exited the conference room. The building's walls were thin, and voices throughout the building seemingly echoed. I heard the president of the panel talking loudly to my supervisor. You can bet things weren't going well for him. Suddenly, the door opened, and my handpicked sponsor walked over to me and said, "Sergeant Payne, you have passed this board and earned your promotion status with a perfect score."

Because I was departing Korea on the very next day, I was instructed to report to the personnel human resources office to pick up a sealed copy of my promotion board proceedings to hand carry to my next duty station. When I arrived, Sergeant First Class Fordham was there along with his entire staff to ensure that my paperwork was correct and properly packaged for my journey. The reason Sergeant First Class Fordham's actions were extraordinary is because it was a weekend.

Fordham directed his entire staff to work on a weekend to ensure that everything was properly assembled for me. I looked at Sergeant First Class Fordham and his team and was amazed. I thought about the extenuating circumstances that led to the moment I was witnessing. Everything I observed represented a special moment in my life. Remarkably and to my pleasure, we are still friends to this day!

Roth "Gus" Allen

My wife is the only girl and youngest of seven siblings. When I met her brothers, one stood out the most. From our very first encounter, we gelled. Sometimes, my wife jokingly asks, "Have you talked to your brother lately?" Roth Allen is my brother-in-law. He goes by the name Gus because he was "almost" born in August. Roth

is a fun-loving, pleasant, and witty guy. I haven't met anyone who has not fallen prey to his down-to-earth disposition.

In 2009, I was initiated into the Omega Psi Phi Fraternity, Incorporated. I've met hundreds, if not thousands, of fraternity brothers. However, becoming a member of a fraternity or other social organizations does not guaranty you'll suddenly acquirer instant friends. Everyone cannot hold the title of friend and will not share your ideology on brotherhood. True friendship will be few and far between. In the 1990s, my

Figure 17. Roth (Gus) Allen in Chicago, Illinois, 2007

brother-in-law and I took trips to Chicago we named "the man weekend." For several years, in the month of August, I looked forward to our trips. We always took this time to talk about the things we wanted for our families, about the future, and we always had loads of fun. If I took one thing from our brotherhood, it would be our ability to dream. I am amazed at how we can sit and talk for hours about things that matter the most to us and how we laugh at life itself. We both share a genuine concern about each other and always want to see the other doing well.

I've had many friends and people who I deeply cared about, but I have yet to experience consistent brotherhood like what I share with my bother-in-law, Gus!

Chapter 4

Permission Granted

For as long as I can remember, I have admired Mr. Denzel Washington. In 2003, his movie *Antwone Fisher* was released on DVD. I was excited about getting the opportunity to watch the movie in support of my favorite actor and his directing debut, especially since I was unable to catch the movie while it was still in the theaters because of my heavy work schedule. Without having a clue about the movie's storyline, I eagerly purchased it after work one evening. After arriving home, my wife and I settled in to watch it together. Straightaway, I picked up on startling parallels between Antwone Fisher's life experiences and my own. Besides the physical and sexual abuse, it was as if I was watching my life being played out before my eyes. The movie stirred up strong emotions deep inside me that I probably had suppressed for nearly thirty years. I couldn't take my eyes off the television as each scene took me deeper and deeper inside myself. There's a part in the movie when Antwone receives acceptance from his biological family. Without saying a word, his elderly grandmother validates his existence and place within the family. By then, I was lying in bed sobbing uncontrollably, leaving my young wife feeling helpless and not knowing what to do or how she could help me through my emotional and psychological breakdown. Until this point in my life, I thought I had everything under control, so this episode left me in an awkward place. My wife and I had several talks about what she witnessed, what I was feeling, and how we would move forward on dealing with what was obviously an invisible hole in my chest that nothing could fill after that point. I've always yearned to know where and from whom I came, but for much of my life, I was very good at deceiving myself about it. I told myself that I was happy and didn't want to know who my biological parents are. Because hindsight is always 20/20, I now know that what was stopping me from opening my Pandora's box was fear, I was so held down by it, I refused to even acknowledge I had a Pandora's box. Of course, I could tell something was missing. My life wasn't empty, I had everything I could ever have asked for, but nothing in life could fill that invisible hole in my chest. I needed answers, but the fear of the unknown kept me from investigating further.

My mother, "the woman who raised me," means the world to me, and I didn't want to do anything to hurt her. I love her more than I can express to her using words. Sometimes, though, all the love in the world is not enough when your inner being desires and thrusts for the truth.

I understood how she felt about the prospect of me finding my biological family. However, that did not stop me from asking for her blessings to pursue the identification of my biological parents.

It took a few days for me to build up the courage to have a critical conversation with my mother about searching my genealogy. When we finally talked, it didn't go as I planned, and she had so many questions that I wasn't prepared to answer. My mother couldn't understand why I needed or wanted to know, and I couldn't formulate the words to combat her confusion. The conversation became too difficult for me to overcome her feelings about why I needed and wanted to know versus my feelings of emptiness. For the sake of stopping the pain for the both of us, I abandoned my need to know and accepted her decision not to support my fact-finding mission on the genealogy of my bloodline.

5,475 Days Later

Fifteen years later, my mother called me and gave me her blessings on searching my genetic lineage. She said, "I prayed about it and thought it's time for you to find your people." My first move was to contact the clerk of courts to obtain a copy of my adoption paperwork. One of the courthouse clerks said, "All adoptions are sealed and are not opened except for non-identifying information such as medical history that may be vital to the adoptee in cases of medical emergency." The clerk also mentioned that both parties to the adoption received a copy of the adoption proceedings from the court when it was finalized.

I shared the information I learned from the court with my mother. Sensing I was about to ask about her copy of the paperwork, she explained to me that earlier in the year while home visiting, she asked me to get an insurance policy from a large purse she kept in the back of her closet. My mother then said to me, "You were holding your adoption papers without realizing it." She went on to explain, while I was rummaging through the purse, my adoption documents were one of the first envelopes that I held in my hand when looking for the insurance policy. Her next admission challenged my patience, understanding, and my very soul in a way that I had never experienced.

She went on to say, "When you left to go home, I destroyed your adoption paperwork because I was scared that you'd find them." Hearing my mother say she destroyed the only copy of my adoption paperwork left me feeling like a part of me was destroyed too. It was a piece of me that I could never get back. For the first time in my life, I felt anger toward my mother. I still loved her deeply. I tried to talk myself into forgiving her. I realized that like me, she too made a decision out of fear. It didn't justify that it was selfish of her, and it took me a few months to forgive her completely and understand the reasons behind her actions. After coming to grips with my disappointment, I picked myself up by the bootstraps and crafted a letter to the Orange County Clerk of Courts. It took a few drafts, but I wanted to provide myself the best opportunity for getting some assistance to help me obtain information about my adoption.

I thought how degrading the entire process was! I was forced to lay down my pride and beg for information that I felt is rightfully mine. The adoption system is designed to protect the confidentiality of the adults with very little future provisions for the babies who grow to become adults without access to vital information that is their own.

My initial draft started out very emotional, and I knew it wouldn't provide me with the best opportunity for receiving a response.

PETITION TO OPEN ADOPTIONS RECORDS CASE NO. CI 76-4882

12/18/2017

• • •

SFC(R) John I. Payne Jr., MBA
108 Brittany Park Road
Columbia, SC 29229
(301) 741-6659
jp0436@gmail.com

Honorable Judge
425 North Orange Avenue
Room 330
Orlando, FL 32801

Honorable Judge

I respectfully petitions the Court for an order, to open my adoption records (CI 76-4882) in its entirety.

I currently reside at 108 Brittany Park Rd, Columbia, SC 29229, however I was born in Orlando, FL on August 9, 1969 where I lived until joining the US Army after graduating high school. During my tenure in the military, I earned an undergraduate and graduate degree. In 1999 I married a beautiful, kind, and loving woman and we have 3 wonderful children together. In 2008, I retired from the US Army after 20 years of Honorable service to our country. I'm currently a Program Analyst with the Department of Veterans Affairs in Washington, D.C. and enrolled at the University of Miami to pursuit a Master of Public Administration. It is my intent to express through this letter my worthiness as a productive citizen and contributor to society. Although there are many, I have thought long and hard as to what reasoning I would give for this request. I was fortunate to be raised by an adopted mother that loved me as if she gave natural birth to me and I hold no resentment towards my biological parents of any form. However, I have a strong desire to learn about my ancestry and hopefully someday discover answers to my life and possibly fill the emptiness of life without genetic mirroring and gain a sense of Family history. I have educated myself, served my country at peace time and at war, Fathered 3 children, and continue to service my country as a federal employee. I selfishly feel that I have earned the right to know who I am, from whom I came from, as well as all the other intangibles that would come from a decision to open my adoption; such as the a possible relationship with my parents, my children meeting their grand-parents, the circumstances of my adoption, family history, medical history, potential siblings, and closer.

Honorable Judge, please rule in my favor and open my adoption files. Your favorable judgement in this matter will be of great help in my effort to fill-in the vacant pieces of my 47 years on this earth as a human-being and honorable servant to society.

Respectfully Yours,

SFC(R) John I. Payne Jr., MBA

Figure 18. Letter to from John Payne to petition the court in 2017

I edited one sentence at a time until I felt it would gain the desired effect I hoped for. After mailing my letter, I received a response from the court, and the judge said she would assign an attorney to open my case and assist with finding my biological mother.

IN THE CIRCUIT COURT OF THE NINTH JUDICIAL CIRCUIT,
IN AND FOR ORANGE COUNTY, FLORIDA

CASE NUMBER: 1976-DR-4882-O

DIVISION 31

IN RE: ADOPTION.

JOHN I. PAYNE, JR.,
Petitioner.

_____/

ORDER APPOINTING INTERMEDIARY

THIS MATTER comes before the Court for consideration of the Petitioner's Motion to Open Sealed Adoption Documents, filed January 23, 2018, in the above-styled case.

The Court hereby appoints Stephen H. Price, Esq., as Intermediary in the above styled cause. Stephen H. Price, Esq. has authority to review the court file for non-identifying and identifying information. Identifying information should not be revealed to a person or entity without further order from the Court.

DONE AND ORDERED in Chambers at Orlando, Orange County, Florida, on this 5th day of February, 2018.

_____
TANYA DAVIS WILSON
CIRCUIT COURT JUDGE

CERTIFICATE OF SERVICE

I HEREBY CERTIFY that a true and correct copy was delivered to the below parties on this 5th day of February, 2018.

John I. Payne, Jr., 108 Brittany Park Road, Columbia, South Carolina 29229
Stephen H. Price, Esq., 1411 Edgewater Drive, Suite 200, Orlando, Florida 32804-6361

_____
Judicial Assistant

Figure 19. Court response to petition 2018

I was beyond ecstatic about the possibilities that awaited me. Once an attorney was assigned, I was optimistic about my chances of finding my biological mother, but after a few weeks, I realized that the help he could provide was limited because his services were pro bono. I have never been the type of person to place all my eggs into one basket, so I submitted my DNA to Ancestry and 23andME, hoping I would receive information that could place me closer to finding out who I am and whom I came from. After submitting my DNA sample, I realized the process is nothing like the law enforcement shows on television. The wait for my results required me to be patient; it was almost unbearable! I also remained in contact with my court-appointed attorney and regularly bombard him with questions about the limitations of our relationship and to gauge what I could get away with in the process.

Finally, my Ancestry account was updated, and before me were hundreds, if not thousands, of individuals who were DNA matches. After roaming around on the Ancestry site for familiarization, I updated my profile with a picture and a short statement that explained my purpose for creating an account. In short order, I received a few messages from people who shared DNA with me and were also on a journey to connect with relatives or gain a better understandings about their lineage.

My first few encounters were the most valuable in helping me understanding how to use other resources, along with Ancestry, to unlock my DNA's full potential. I began researching all things DNA to ensure I didn't overlook anything that might be valuable in assisting me with finding my biological mother. One of the most important terms I needed to understand was centimorgans. In genetic genealogy, a centimorgan (cM) or map unit (m.u.) is a unit of recombinant frequency which is used to measure genetic distance and is used to predict the degree of relationship statistically (ISOGG Wiki [January 2, 2019], centimorgan, http://isogg.org/wiki/CentiMorgan).

Percentage	cMs Shared	Relationship
50%	3400	Parent/child
50%	2550	Siblings (see the Shaping DNA with Siblings sidebar)
25%	1700	Grandfather, grandmother, aunt, uncle, niece, nephew, half-siblings
12.50%	850	Great-grandparent, first cousin, great-uncle/aunt, half-uncle/aunt
6.25%	425	First cousin once removed
3.13%	212.5	Second cousin
1.56%	106.25	Second cousin once removed
0.78%	53.13	Third cousin

Figure 20. Centimorgan relationship chart

Karl Henry

Figure 21. Karl Henry

When I logged into my Ancestry account, I found several DNA matches listed according to the amount of centimorgans we shared and from highest to lowest. Karl Henry was the first name listed. Because I was new to Ancestry, I was very nervous and almost scared to contact anyone right away, but my concerns quickly faded. I wanted to know more about Karl, and I used any and every information platform I could find to do so.

Armed with my laptop and something to write with, I conducted a deep dive into Karl's background and found he's from Florida and we share some of the same physical characteristics. I can only speculate how most people feel when they look at their relatives.

I think many people take for granted the experience of genetic mirroring their entire lives, but for me, it's extraordinary! Besides the amount of centimorgans Karl and I share, we both enlisted in and retired from the U.S. Army. As an army recruiter, I made many cold calls to people I didn't personally know. Therefore, I felt it would be easy to initiate a call to Karl. Boy, was I wrong! This call was different, and my training didn't prepare me for initiating a call to someone I am genetically connected to. Several thoughts ran through my mind including rejection and whether the person on the other end would be as open to exploring our genealogical connection with the same level of interest as me.

After a few days of grappling with my fears and questions, I dialed Karl's number and waited for someone to answer. To my surprise, he was very receptive and willing to share information about his biological lineage. The information Karl shared with me proved to be extremely helpful to me as I continued deeper into my biological journey. After much research, I have come to believe Karl may very well be my maternal uncle, but we haven't been successful in confirming our relationship.

Ferguson[2]

A young lady name Tanya was my second highest DNA match on Ancestry. She is from Miami, Florida, and we share 375 centimorgans between us, which means we are first cousins. By now, the entire Ancestry search process had become overwhelming, and I had to dig for even more courage to reach out to her in search of information about my biological mother.

On December 13, 2017, I sent Tanya an e-mail asking if she would be willing to share access to her Ancestry family tree and if she would also be willing to exchange information between us, although I didn't feel I had anything of value to offer her. Tanya replied to my e-mail and shared her hypothesis on how we are related. She was extremely confident that our DNA connection was through her maternal side of the family. Tanya shared the surnames of her maternal family—Ferguson and Collie.

As I continued receiving e-mails from Tanya, she explained that her grandparents were first-generation Americans from the Bahamas.

Figure 22. Dinner at Tanya's home 2019

The confidence, pride, and strength of her words resonated deep inside me because I knew, at that point, the ancestry connection between us was strong. I gained a better understanding about her certainty of why we were related on her maternal side. Tanya's father is Caucasian, so my search became easier because I was able to narrow it to her maternal side of the family. This information made it possible for me to more easily find one, if not both, of my biological parents. Throughout December 2017, Tanya and I shared lots of information by e-mail.

I made several requests for her phone number because I felt it was a more effective and efficient form of communication. Out of nowhere one Saturday afternoon, Tanya called me! She told me she had her cousin on the line too. Tanya's cousin and I are members of the same college fraternity. And out of a sense of obligation, it appeared, he understood how important finding my biological parents was to me, and he wanted to assist me in any way that he could. They both had several questions for me before Tanya explained her anxiety over the amount of DNA we share. Because I was a neophyte to the Ancestry community, several months passed before I came to understand what I felt Tanya already assumed about our biological connection.

The whole thing was puzzling because of the close match between us and the lack of a DNA match between her cousin and me. Tanya and I are confirmed first cousins, which was visible to both of us on Ancestry. To assist me, Tanya and her cousin shared information with me about their elders. As the call ended, Tanya put me on notice, saying she would not dedicate any of her time toward assisting me with research. Her tone and the matter-of-fact way in which she spoke made me laugh. At that moment, I instantly knew, without a shadow of doubt, that we were related. Not only would I have said what she said in the same way, but also I would have said it with the same amount of attitude. Tanya did agree to continue sharing information she came across with me, and I promised to do the same.

Curt Parks II

Curtis Parks II was my third highest DNA match. His profile was instrumental in helping me crack the code on the paternal side of my family. His family tree provided me with a wealth of information that painted a vivid picture of where I fit in on a family tree with lots of branches. Because Curt is the offspring of an interracial marriage, it allowed me the assurance to focus predominantly on one side of his family tree, just as I did with Tanya.

Figure 23. Curt Parks II

Aside from the amount of DNA between us, we shared a lot in common. My research unveiled his level of drive, entrepreneurial endeavors, and intelligence that shined through the information I found. Much of what I found answered many of the questions I had about myself and explained my interests in entrepreneurship. On paper, Curt checked all the appropriate boxes as a man and as a productive citizen. He is educated, world-traveled, and shows signs of intellectual curiosity as he moved throughout life on his terms. He graduated from the University of North Carolina at Chapel Hill, University of Miami at Coral Gables, and is a member of what I believe to be the most celebrated African American Greek fraternity in the world, Omega Psi Phi, Fraternity, Incorporated.

Conducting research on my unknown relative provided me a sense of pride to be a part of premium stock, although I had not met him nor knew how we were related.

Eugene and Anthony Lewis

Figure 24. Eugene Lewis

Several weeks after receiving my first set of DNA matches, another one was posted to my account. By now, I had a relatively solid understanding of how Ancestry makes genetic linkage, but my new match created feelings of disbelief, excitement, and very mixed emotions. Yes, I understood what the information was showing me about the relationship between my DNA and the new match, but I found it hard to believe. This can't be possible! If what I am seeing is correct, I have a sibling! Man, this was a possibility I could have never imagined because as far as I knew I was an only child.

I needed more information! I needed someone to explain what my new but unbelievable DNA match meant, so I called Ancestry. The representative I spoke to provided me with information on the different variations of the match, and I concluded that it meant only one thing; but still in disbelief, I now have a biological brother!

His profile on Ancestry didn't have a photograph, but his small family tree did list the names of his father, grandmother, and an uncle.

Figure 25. Anthony Lewis

Anthony Lewis was my new and closest DNA match, but this was a name I was sure I had never heard before.

I replayed my entire childhood in my mind as if watching a movie in fast-forward, but I couldn't connect him to any moment in my past. I looked through every school yearbook and still nothing! I tried to make contact with Anthony several times via Ancestry messages, but my attempts went unanswered. Through further research, I was able to obtain contact information for Mr. Eugene Lewis, the person listed on Anthony's family tree as his father. Being able to talk with Mr. Lewis posed a small problem for me because he lived in a different time zone. To complicate matters even more, during this time, I commuted for work from Columbia, South Carolina, to Washington, DC, along with honoring my obligations as a father, husband, and student pursuing a second graduate degree. Talking about being overwhelmed, I was feeling it! I reached out to Mr. Lewis, and eventually, he agreed to speak with me. He provided me with valuable information that placed me one step closer to finding my biological mother. Mr. Lewis and I talked for hours. He provided information about the big brother I didn't know and had never met. Through our conversation, I learned that Mr. Lewis and I graduated from the same high school, and like me, he also served in the military.

After sharing much about his life with me, I was convinced that he was not my biological father. Mr. Lewis allowed me to ask him questions that helped me connect some of the puzzle pieces in my journey to unravel the complicated web of deception my biological mother—I'm sure—wanted deeply buried, but I was determined to figure it out; I needed to know where and from whom I came from.

Just before our call neared an end, Mr. Lewis mentioned that Anthony's mother's name is Sarah Harris. Hmm, this was different from what I believed my biological mother's name is. He also shared that he heard Sarah had given birth to another child a few years after I was born.

I thanked Mr. Lewis for accepting my call, answering my questions, and for providing me with such valuable information. He asked me to keep him updated on my progress, and we ended our call knowing that we'd talk again soon. Our conversation gave me a lot of hope.

Eddie (Uncle-Daddy) Harris, Jr.

Figure 26. Dr. Eddie L. Harris, Jr.

After several attempts to reach Anthony and conversations with Mr. Lewis, I turned my attention to Eddie, Anthony's uncle. To my advantage, I found a wealth of information on the Internet about Eddie which made it much easier for me to track him down. During my research, I learned Eddie is a retired pastor and member of the same fraternity as me, which I hoped would work in my favor when I reach out to him. Eddie Harris, Jr. had recently published a book, and I was instantly impressed with the many articles I read about his achievements in the very city I was born and raised. He was also involved in local politics and had a hand in many of the initiatives to improve living conditions for those of us who lived in public housing throughout Orlando. Eddie also mentored several young people in the community and was heavily involved in the local community college in the 1980s. The deeper I researched into his background, the more information I found that referenced his many contributions in our hometown. I was unsure of our exact relationship, but I remember sitting in my home office thinking how much I had achieved over the years, yet I fell extremely short of Eddie's documented achievements that are available to anyone to discover if they so elect to research his amazing legacy.

Figure 27. Overcoming the Fear of Flying authored by Dr. Eddie Harris, Jr.

Chapter 5

The Spit Don't Lie

My mother shared with me the only piece of information she could recall at the time. She provided me with what she believed was the name of my birth mother, and it was a name that I will never forget: Mary Alice Martin.

After gathering enough information to ensure that I was on the right path before contacting Eddie Harris, I thought about the method I would use to reach out to him and considered what I would say once I did. I finally settled on the use of an e-mail to establish my initial contact. I knew that I had to craft my words wisely to get an answer, and after doing so, I sent the e-mail to him and patiently awaited his response. Amazingly enough, I didn't have to wait long because Eddie called. During our conversation, I explained who I was or at least who I thought I was and told him why I wanted to speak with him. I told Eddie that I had a long talk with Mr. Lewis, who is Anthony's father, and asked if he knew either of them. Eddie responded, "I know them both." He confirmed that Anthony was his nephew and Mr. Lewis was, in fact, Anthony's father.

Deacon Franklin "Franco" Harris

Before I could explore any deeper into my biological lineage, Eddie told me that his brother, Frank, passed away earlier that day and he needed time to mourn his death. I offered him my condolences, and we set a time shortly after the funeral to resume our conversation. When the call ended, I quickly investigated the name Frank Harris and was amazed at my findings. For example, the resemblance we shared. Thoughts ran through my mind like a gazelle. I asked myself, "Am I too late? Is Frank my father?" The many thoughts were taxing! After the funeral, Eddie and I reconnected as promised. Looking back, the funeral gave me time to organize my notes and to develop an order for the questions I hoped Eddie could answer. When we resumed, I asked

Figure 28. Frank Harris

Eddie if he would be willing to submit to a DNA test to determine how we are related. Surprisingly, he readily agreed. Eddie and I continued to communicate daily while we waited for the results to be posted to my Ancestry account. Through our daily conversations, we formed an unbreakable bond, and the similarities between us were undeniable.

Both of us were uncertain about our family ties; however, through the process of elimination, we decided that he could only be my biological father or uncle. Jokingly, I called him Uncle-Daddy, and he affectionately responded, "Nephew-son." Before long, his results were posted, and it was official: Eddie Harris, Jr. is my biological maternal uncle. However, he will forever be my Uncle-Daddy!

Sarah's Baby Boy

I told my Uncle Eddie that Mr. Lewis mentioned he believed Sarah had a child a few years after I was born, and I wanted to know if the information he provided was accurate. Uncle Eddie confirmed the accuracy of Mr. Lewis's information, and he also provided me with the name of Sarah's youngest son, Corey. On that very evening, I went to work on finding anything I could about my little brother. I questioned myself repeatedly, "Another son?" I worked late into the night and burned through every resource available to me in my search for Corey until I fell asleep.

While still exhausted from the night before, I got up early on the next morning and continued my research with the zeal of a mad scientist. At one point, my wife picked up my high school yearbook and walked over to me. She held the yearbook out and said, "Look." Still more focused on what I was doing, I dismissively glanced at the photograph she was pointing to and said, "Yeah, that's Corey. We were in JROTC together during my senior year."

My wife then said, "Look again!"

Figure 29. Cory Fallings, Jr. year and John Payne, Jr.
Sr. Year at Jones High school Orlando, Florida

Acting on her direction, I looked at the photograph again and couldn't believe my eyes, believing I had lived without genetic mirroring for forty-eight years and there it was right in front of me. Instantly, I could see Corey and I are somehow related, yet I remained doubtful!

Several weeks before receiving Uncle Eddie's results, my wife and I planned our annual vacation to Orlando, Florida. On the next morning after we arrived, I called Uncle Eddie to let him know I was in town and that I hoped to see him while there. I felt that I needed to interact with a blood relative for the first time in my life. Earlier in the week, I learned Uncle Eddie shared his mornings with a few local guys at McDonald's, and one of the gentlemen is the father of a classmate and the son-in-law of the bishop at the church I attended while growing up. My wife accompanied me to McDonald's to meet Uncle Eddie for the first time in person. As we ate our breakfast, the three of us talked about everything, it was a joy to be in his presence. When the time came to leave, I really felt that I needed more time with my new uncle, but my wife and I had obligations to our children as it was our annual winter vacation when my wife and I spend quality time with our children in Orlando, and leave the cold winter weather of the northern states behind.

Early that evening, my wife and I decided to take the kids to see the Blue Man Show at Universal Studios Orlando. I asked her if my new uncle could join us. Without hesitation, she said, "Yes, absolutely!"

The anticipation of spending time with someone from my side of the family excited me. In fact, I was as excited as when I was a kid waiting for my dad to take me to the Central Florida Fair. I thought, this will be the first time my children will meet a biological relative from my side of the family, how amazing!

Figure 30. The Payne family meeting Eddie L. Harris
for the first time in Orlando, Florida, 2018

Once all of us were together, the love that flowed between us was instantaneous! It was as if we shared many moments together long before that day, and my kids were quickly drawn to Uncle Eddie as if they had known him their entire lives. I watched my oldest son interact with him as though there was no time lost between them. At one point, Uncle Eddie talked about the strong resemblance between my daughter and his sister. Like all good vacations, they come to an end and this one was no different.

After my family and I returned home, I continued my research from where I left off. When I logged into my Ancestry account, I noticed a message from a DNA match at the cousin level who shared her contact information and asked that I call her. After a few minutes of small talk and feeling each other out, Tonya Lynel moved the conversation to her purpose for contacting me. She talked about the amount of time she spent on genealogical research and what she hoped to gain from her Ancestry membership. Tonya also discussed her thoughts about our biological connection and then asked, "Have you ever heard of an old school R&B group named, Sam & Dave?" I couldn't remember anything about the group at the time. To jar my memory, she sang a few words from "Hold on I'm Coming" and "Soul Man," two of their 1960s hits.

I told her, "I vaguely recall their popularity but not much of anything else." Tonya then mentioned Dave Prater, one half of the music duo, was a descendant of her family, and I too was related to him.

I'm a Soul Man

After our call ended, I quickly logged in to my Ancestry account to review my shared matches. I wanted to determine whether I was really related to Dave Prater on either side of my family tree. My research confirmed that I am related to the Prater family through my maternal bloodline. I called Uncle Eddie to ask if he knew about his ties to Dave Prater. His response was very enlightening and caused the fire within me to burn even brighter.

He told me about a time in the 1960s when his father introduced him to Dave Prater during a session break at one of his performances.

He spoke about the happiness he felt when Dave sat at the table with his father and him and acknowledged them as family. Further research proved that I am the third cousin to Dave Prater, which means Uncle Eddie is the second cousin and his mother, a first cousin. Researching my history became an obsession, and the more I learned about my lineage, the better I felt about who I am as a person. I started to walk just a little bit taller, and my pores secreted pride.

As I continued down the rabbit hole of researching my family history on the Internet, I discovered an annual music festival that honored the R&B music legend Dave Prater in his hometown of Ocilla, Georgia. I remember going to work and playing the hits of Sam & Dave softly in my cubical and sharing my heritage with my coworkers. Later that week, I called Uncle Eddie to ask if he ever attended the festival and if he would like to go. He readily accepted my invitation, and we made plans to

Figure 31. Ocilla Festival 2018

attend the Ocilla's Soul Man Festival, which would be a first for the both of us. I went to work on planning our trip. The logistics proved challenging because Uncle Eddie lived in Florida, and I resided in South Carolina at the time. I agreed to fly him to South Carolina, and then we would drive to Georgia for the festival. I was extremely excited about our trip. I was also certain it would provide an opportunity to get to know him better and possibly obtain more answers to my unanswered questions.

The day was fast approaching, and I could only imagine how much fun Uncle Eddie and I would have when he arrived. This was new territory for me because I had never shared my personal space with anyone from my side of the family.

Uncle Eddie finally arrived, I drove to the airport to pick him up, and we then returned home. Uncle Eddie settled himself into the house and then joined me outside on the front porch. I felt amazing! My biological uncle, frat brother, and friend was sitting alongside me in South Carolina. We talked about several things and enjoyed the warm weather. I was bubbling over with joy and pride, as I had made right on a promise to myself to be victorious in my pursuit of finding genetically related family. We continued to sit on the porch, and without a word uttered, I could tell that he was proud of me and my

Figure 32. John and Eddie sitting on John's front porch in South Carolina, 2018

accomplishments, despite knowing his sister, for reasons unknown, gave me up for adoption at birth. An occasional neighbor passed by in a car and waved, and we returned the customary country wave of the hand to all those who passed by.

The next morning, we set out on the drive to Ocilla, Georgia. I can't tell you how many miles we traveled or the duration of the trip because we laughed and joked every single mile and every minute of the way. All the questions I wanted to ask no longer carried any merit because I was living in the moment, and it felt natural as if it was supposed to be.

Figure 33. Eddie Harris and John Payne at First Baptist in Ocilla, GA 2018

Every action and reaction, jester, and word were from a place of love. For me, there was no doubt in my mind that I was in the presence of someone of my lineage. We share the same taste in clothes, jokes, as well as likes and dislikes. Eddie was the closest match to my personality that I'd ever encountered in my entire life. We arrived in Ocilla and prepared ourselves for the worship service. It served as the kick off for the weekend festivities and was held in an old wooden country church where Dave Prater grew up singing in the choir. I could honestly tell that little had changed since Dave Prater last sang in that very church. As Uncle Eddie and I sat in the old wooden pews, it was evident that we were outsiders, and because we arrived early, some of the family members began asking questions about who we were.

Figure 34. Mary Lee (Prater) Traylor-Harris

I sat back, and Uncle Eddie spoke for the both of us. After the benediction, we were acknowledged by the family, and Dave's sisters invited us to breakfast at one of their homes the next morning. When we arrived at Dave Prater's sister's home, we were welcomed with open arms. I was sitting in the living room of a relative who was the sister of an R&B Hall of Fame inductee and relative of mine. The room was filled with his memorabilia and reminded me of being in a museum. There were photographs and other objects associated with Dave. I felt elated to know that I was somewhere down the branch of such a magnificent family tree. Because I am an adoptee, nothing concerning my biological connections is overlooked nor taken for granted. During an open conversation at breakfast, the sisters of Dave Prater shared their condolences about the loss of my grandmother and the mother of Uncle Eddie, Ms. Mary Lee (Prater) Traylor-Harris. They reminisced about the times they shared with their cousin and my grandmother Mary. I could see my Uncle Eddie moved to joy as our elder cousins spoke highly about his mother. We enjoyed our breakfast which, in my opinion, rivaled any quick service restaurant in the western hemisphere. Uncle Eddie began telling the four Prater sisters the story of how I tracked down my relatives through DNA and research.

At one point, he said, "He can tell his story a lot better than I can," and everyone in the room looked at me to continue where Uncle Eddie left off. When I finished my story, one of the Prater sisters said she found my journey incredible, and it was something that you rarely hear about in everyday life; just on television shows about adoption or researching family history.

A daughter of a Prater sister had taken the responsibility of compiling their family history, and she placed a few boxes on the table and began to share the family history with everyone in the room. One of the elder Prater sisters began sharing more information about the Prater family and Dave's childhood.

I felt a lot like Antwone Fisher in the moment he was accepted into the family by his grandmother at the end of the movie. Uncle Eddie and I so richly enjoyed our time with Dave Prater's sisters, and what we took away was worth more than gold. The time came for us to leave Ocilla, Georgia, just as we came, laughing and joking the entire way back to South Carolina. On the next morning after returning home, I made my way to the airport to ensure Uncle Eddie didn't miss his flight back to Orlando. Once he was checked in, we said our goodbyes as if we weren't going to see each other for a long time. I hugged him and said, "Goodbye, Uncle-Daddy."

And he then said, "Goodbye, Nephew-Son."

Figure 35. (l to r) Janie Poole, Bertha McMath, Lillie Demps, and Helen DeBerry. Sister of Dave Prater.

As I walked back to my truck, it felt as if parts of me were falling from my body. I sat in the parking lot until his scheduled departure passed. Not only that, I needed time to gather my emotions.

Three Miles Apart

A few days after our trip to Ocilla, the perfect movement of God was revealed to me again. On the morning of Sunday, April 22, 2018, the DNA results for Corey were posted to Ancestry. Corey and I share 1,878 centimorgans across 94 DNA segments.

If you've been following along with the story, I'm sure this will be of no surprise, Corey and I are brothers! You cannot imagine the happiness blended with some amount of confusion I felt about having another brother. Even before the results were posted, I felt as if I should have known we were brothers back in the late 1980s during the two school years we shared at the same high school. I stared at his yearbook picture again, and I couldn't help but think that I received a small amount of genetic mirroring during my high school years without knowing. I dug into my memory and was able to recall the many times our paths had crossed in school, particularly during my senior year when he was my JROTC Company Commander. I always thought about how much we resembled each other.

Unsure if Corey had seen the results, I carefully drafted a text message to notify my little brother about the results. Unlike the other results I received, Corey's was more confirmation than surprise. Both of us suspected the results would turn out the way they did. However, once his result was posted, it caused me to believe my lying eyes. I then began to believe definitively that Mary Alice Martin and Sarah Lee Harris are one in the same. It was hard for me to come to grips with the different name. I had become fixated on the name I had come to believe was the correct name. My disbelief caused me to create a diagram to feed my visual preference of learning and made things clear for me to except.

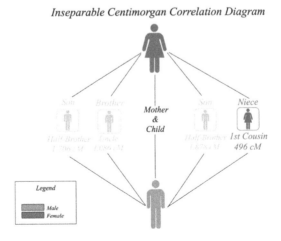

Figure 36. Inseparable Centimorgan Correlation Diagram

All my maternal connections led to one individual. Considering all the facts, she was the only woman that could have given birth to me. Eddie Harris, Jr. was tested and confirmed as my uncle. In addition, he had only one sister. Anthony was tested, and he was proven to be my half brother, and Corey's results followed suit. The icing on the cake was Latonya, she is one of Sarah's nieces and my first cousin who was confirmed not only by the DNA, but my uncle also established the legitimacy of her relationship to us both.

The woman who raised me has never lied to me. She is the textbook definition of integrity, and I couldn't disregard her words as inaccurate. The only conclusion I could draw was Sarah consciously used a false name when she gave me up for adoption. Even more alarming to me, a person can get away with using a false name in the court's adoption process in the 1960s; therefore, the court's adoption process was greatly flawed. If my assumption were indeed factual, this meant that Sarah went through great lengths to conceal my birth and her identity. These actions forced me to exhaust all means to gather enough evidence in preparation for the encounter I hoped to have with my birth mother someday.

I focused all the energy I had left on composing an email to my court-appointed attorney to share what I had uncovered. After sending the e-mail to him, I soon developed a strategy to flush Sarah out of hiding, which I hoped would allow me the opportunity to meet her in person. The attorney and I discussed possible days, as well as times of the day that may be better for contacting her. I explained to him how I had made several attempts to contact my biological mother without receiving any response. I was hoping that as a court-appointed attorney, he could shake her up enough that she would at least respond to a call from someone on my behalf. Several weeks had passed when Sarah finally responded to my attorney and he contacted me soon thereafter. My court-appointed attorney explained that Sarah stated she had no interest in meeting me. Of course, there are no laws currently in place that can compel her to sit down with me.

The news was disturbing, painful, and difficult for me to accept her position after so much hard work, persistence, and praying to get to this point and not get the opportunity to meet my birth mother face-to-face. Although I had figured out who my birth mother is, I was still far away from what I considered to be the crown jewel of my efforts.

Once the decision was made, I was all in on the goal that I set for myself. I would not accept nothing short of meeting my birth mother and gain answers to all the questions I had pondered for almost fifty years. However, because my birth mother used a false name, I was able to prove her identity through DNA, and this made room for me to receive a copy of my adoption file un-redacted. Once I received my file in the mail, the very first document after a letter from the appointed attorney was my original birth certificate. I stared at it for a while and listened to the story the document told. The name on my birth certificate was left blank; this meant my birth mother failed to name me before placing me into adoption. My original birth certificate caused me an emotional imbalance; my feelings were split down the middle. I was excited to view my original birth certificate for the first time; it made me feel as if I had gained a small part of my being. But on the other hand, I felt sorrow and somehow thrown away by the woman who gave birth to me. Not because I was adopted, rather because she did not think enough of me to give me a name.

No Response

By this time, I had gained much more than I initially set out to achieve. I now had two brothers and an uncle that I was unaware of before my search for my birth mother began.

However, my search and geological discovery was far from complete. I found myself more frequently in deep thought about how I would move forward in my pursuit to meet my birth mother and ask her questions about my adoption. After confirming the identity of my birth mother, I sat down and composed a letter to formally reintroduce myself to the woman who gave birth to me almost fifty years ago. I hoped she would create a small amount of space in her heart to allow us to form something resembling a relationship. Because so much time had passed, I was not disillusioned in my thinking as if we would start a mother-son relationship because my rearing had

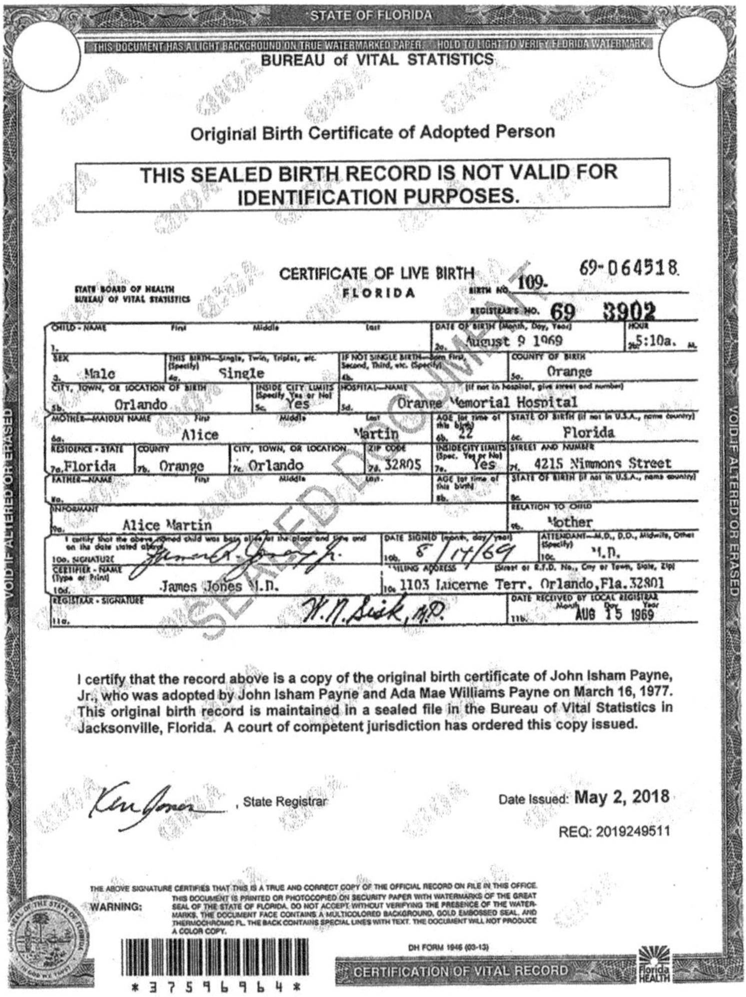

*Figure 37. Certified copy of original birth certificate
of John Payne before adoption*

already taken place so long ago. But I hoped we could build an adult relationship based on honesty and friendship.

As I wrote my letter something strange started happening to me, the sorrow and sadness that I had for myself dissipated. Once I proofread my letter, I began to think what it would be like to have held a secret for nearly fifty years. I thought about the internal cancer-like damage such a heavy and emotionally buried decision to give up a child that was conceived from an illegitimate relationship must be. For me, none of that mattered, but I could not help but feel sorry for my birth mother as if she had been hiding in her dark personal closet, afraid to share with the world the birth of her second born son. I imagined what life must have been like for her in the late 1960s and how society would have condemned and ostracized her within her own community.

After mailing my letter, I waited with great anticipation hoping she would respond in some fashion. But she remained silent, tightly clutching on to her confidentiality—her deeply held and surely draining secret even though the cat was completely out of the bag. Once she read my letter, she contacted Uncle Eddie to ask him to meet her for lunch.

She wanted to discuss my letter with him. This was refreshing news to me because it confirmed that she had received and read the letter I worked so hard to get just right.

April 18, 2018

Hello Sarah Lee (Harris) Fallings,

My name is John I. Payne Jr. and I was born August 9, 1969. Before I ask my one request of you, I want to share with you how I came to this point. About five months ago I submitted my DNA to Ancestry and my first closest match was your son, Anthony Lewis. After an intense search, I found your brother, Eddie Lee Harris Jr. Eddie agreed to take a DNA test and his results came back as my uncle. Continued research revealed that Anthony has a half-brother name Corey Van Fallings, born in 1971. Corey was very easy to track down because we attended the same high school during the 1987/88 school years; he was also in my high school yearbook. After speaking with Corey, he also agreed to take a DNA test and his DNA results to return, a young lady by the name of LaTonya (Dupree) Dillard showed up on Ancestry as a 1st cousin match. It did not take me long to determine that she is your brother's daughter, Mr. James Dupree. So, there you have it!

As for me, the woman who raised me, "my mother", was and is a wonderful woman. She provided me with an outstanding childhood filled with unconditional love, patience, and understanding. Most importantly, my mother raised me with strong Christian values and beliefs that has made me the man I am today.

After graduating high school, I enlisted in the US Army and retired honorably after 20 years of service. Currently, I am a Program Analyst with the Federal government working for the Department of Veterans Affairs in our nation's capital. I also hold a Bachelor of Science in Business Administration, a Master of Business Administration, and currently pursuing another master's degree in Public Administration from the University of Miami. I am a husband of 20 years and also, a father of three beautiful children. In fact, my youngest child and only daughter bears a striking resemblance to you!

My reason for sharing that information with you was to nail home the fact that I do not want anything! However, there is something that I need. I need to know the name of my biological father. If you can find it in your heart to grant me this one request, I will honor your wishes and never attempt to contact you again. Time is our greatest resource and none of us know how much of it we have left. If you do not wish to speak with me directly, please email me at [redacted].com or provide the information to someone else and have them make contact with me. I can be reached anytime day or night, via email or at (███) ███-████.

Thanks in advance.
John I. Payne Jr.

Figure 38. A letter written by John Payne, Jr. to initiate contact with his birth mother

I was able to share my feelings with my uncle and what I hoped to accomplish by sending my letter. I hoped he would relay my message of good will and express to my birth mother that I harbored no animosity towards her or about being adopted. My only wish, as it pertained to her, was to see her face and maybe ask a few uncomfortable questions. I felt that I had accomplished much in life and was deserving of the opportunity to see, with my own eyes, the woman who birthed me into this world. After my birth mother and uncle met for lunch, I could hardly wait to hear about their conversation. Later that evening, I was able to talk with my uncle about their conversation. My letter did not garner the affect I desired and hoped for. Apparently, my birth mother blamed her brother for what she believed was a series of unfortunate events with the emergence of her adopted son. She blamed him for information that I obtained about her and those around her. My uncle tried to explain to her that once I began to reach out to my maternal lineage, I was merely confirming my research and had already done my due diligence as it related to her. All was not lost; my birth mother did confirm to my uncle that she did give birth to me. She also had a very difficult time coming to grips with the fact that I had found her. Along with me finding her, she could not comprehend why I felt the need to know who she was to me. For me, this was refreshing news, and although my letter did not yield the desired effect I hoped for, it did set my emotions at ease because she did not outright renounce my existence all together. My uncle and I ended our conversation, both totally confused about her stance on me finding her and her unwillingness to accept my request to meet with her in person. All my life, I wondered about how it felt to have a sibling because I was raised as an only child. Now I felt like I was destroying the relationship between my uncle and his sister with my probes for acceptance or at least acknowledgment from the very woman who didn't have the desire to act as a parent to me in the first place.

Chapter 6

My First Supper

> *I believe that much like how a pilot loads a plane's computer with all of the necessary flight data that it needs to fly itself, God, in the same way, does that exact same thing with each of us through His DNA—Divine Nurturing of the Almighty!*
> —Pastor Eddie Harris, Jr.

The DNA had spoken. My birth mother's side of the family was no longer a mystery to me. I could account for three generations of my maternal side of the family, and I was on the way to discovering even more about them, but I hadn't met any of them, except my maternal uncle who I affectionately call Uncle-Daddy.

Uncle-Daddy suggested having a dinner in my hometown of Orlando, Florida, so I could meet my maternal relatives. Without hesitation, I agreed and expressed my excitement about being able to interact with my material relatives for the first time in my life. After we arranged the dinner, I discussed the meet and greet dinner with my wife. Immediately thereafter, we made plans to hit the road for what turned into a seven-hour road trip. My family and I arrived in Orlando safely, and the level of my excitement was extremely high.

The evening before the dinner, I felt like a child on Christmas Eve. I tossed and turned in bed, and I couldn't even go to sleep. It was as if I was awaiting Santa's arrival like a child. I recall feeling sick to my stomach because I hadn't disclosed with the real reason for coming home to my mother. I don't believe that I was dishonest with her either. I simply felt that I couldn't share my real reason for coming home because I feared having to answer the many questions my mother may have which I was not mentally prepared to answer.

The Drive-By

After learning where my birth mother lived, I thought about the many times I drove through her neighborhood as a teenager. Once I arrived home, I couldn't help but marvel over the fact that during most of my childhood, I was raised only three miles away from the woman who gave birth to me. I was overwhelmed with curiosity, and it was imperative that I see with my own eyes where she lived. I typed her address into my trucks GPS and set out to find her house.

When I made it to her street, I drove slowly to ensure that I didn't miss my opportunity to gaze at where she live, not sure of the benefits, if any, I would gain by doing so. Because the street ended in a cul-de-sac, I had a second chance to ride slowly pass her home. Although I wanted to pull into the driveway and knock on the door, I reframed from doing so and kept driving by. Oddly, I felt like I committed a criminal act by simply driving past my birth mother's house without her knowledge.

Suppertime

My family and I got dressed for dinner early because I wanted to ensure that we arrived well ahead of schedule. It was very important to me to make a good first impression. I also wanted to ensure that my new family understood how important our first meeting was to me and that I wasn't taking it lightly. With my pushing and rushing, my family and I arrived early at the mall where the restaurant was located.

My nerves were on constant edge, so I walked around the mall to calm myself before everyone else arrived.

Figure 39. (l to r) Kim Harris, Eddie Harris, and Callie Harris

While walking around, I received a call form Uncle-Daddy who told me he had arrived, so we met inside the mall. Of course, my wife took advantage of some retail therapy while Uncle-Daddy and I meandered through the mall. When we were all inside the restaurant, our tables were not ready because of the size of our group, so we were forced to start our meet and greet outside of the restaurant, in the walkway leading into the mall.

Uncle-Daddy asked me, "Are you all right?" He sensed my attempts to manage my level of anxiety. After all, I was meeting my maternal relatives for the very first time. In that moment, I was dealing with so many emotions; so to break the ice, I offered my new male cousins a round of drinks. While at the bar, the walls of unfamiliarity began to slowly come down.

My cousins and I laughed and enjoyed each other's company. I recall Uncle-Daddy's son asking me, "Why did you get all the height?" It became clear to me that he too was attempting to break the ice on what was obviously new and uncomfortable territory for all of us. Because of my adoption, I was hidden in plain sight from my maternal family for forty-nine years. I was estranged and recall feeling like a circus side show during the meet and greet. I felt like a unicorn, and my newfound biological relatives were not going to miss their opportunity to view something that didn't really exist. They could not believe their aunt had such a large skeleton in her closet. One of my birth mother's nieces mentioned how disappointed she was at her aunt.

Apparently, she had been on the opposite end of a religious conversation with my birth mother about living as a Christian. My birth mother, having a secret son who seemingly had emerged out of thin air, appeared to be very hypocritical to say the least.

*Figure 40. (l to r) Eddie Harris, Patrick Harris, and
John Payne first dinner with maternal family*

Uncle Eddie's children shouldered the bulk of the attendance at the meet-and-greet dinner, which I later coined the first supper. I thought about the biblical story of Jesus and the last supper, not to compare myself to him in any way. I envisioned the portrait of Jesus sitting at the center of the table with his disciples seated left and right. I began experiencing a new set of foreign emotions that rushed me all at once. Along with these emotions came a wide variety of questions, such as, will they accept me? How do they feel about me discovering them and possibly interrupting the status quo of what they knew life to be before I attached myself to the family tree? I found myself attempting to host the dinner to hide my anxiety and level of awareness about the situation. I needed to capture as much of the moment as I could in my memory and by pictures, so I moved from table to table talking and requesting to take pictures. I could tell that other than my wife, children, and Uncle-Daddy, none of the others fully understood the level of importance this meeting meant to me.

I truly believe all of us were there for a different reason. I was there to meet and connect with the family I was deprived of knowing, as well as to take in as much genetic mirroring as I could identify.

After reading the article *Happy Adoptee* by Julie A. Rist, I became hypersensitive to genetic mirroring and searched for it for many years, but I no longer needed to look as it was now among me. Moments during the dinner took me back in time to a past family reunion with my adopted family. The atmosphere was the same but different in one simple way, I was among people from my family tree, and somewhere on this tree is a branch of my own.

The Ride Down

As the evening came to an end, we said our goodbyes. I decided to introduce Uncle-Daddy to my adoptive mother for the first time. As we exited the restaurant, I also decided to ride with him, and my wife would meet us back at my adoptive mother's house. As Uncle-Daddy and I drove away, I did something reminiscent of what John Payne, Sr. used to do. It took me back to when he used to ask to stop at the All-Boys College, a local ABC liquor store, to purchase his beverage of choice. I saw a 7-Eleven convenience store off in the distance and asked Uncle Eddie to stop so that I could get something to calm my nerves.

At the time, I felt I needed a menthol cigarette to help me through the evening. When I walked out of the 7-Eleven, I could hardly wait to light up and inhale the menthol deep into my lungs. As I drew the smoke into my lungs, I could feel its calming effects on my nerves. It seemed just the right antidote for dealing with forty-nine years of emotion crammed into one dinner. When I got back into the car, Uncle-Daddy gave me a short but effective lecture on quitting smoking. He painted a vivid picture about the exhaustive effort I had exerted and the hard work I had successfully completed only to be undone at the end of a cigarette. He also spoke about the importance of my role within my immediate family mainly due to the loss of my wife's parents earlier that year. His ability to reach me on a caring and real level was reassuring of our genetic connection. I had never experienced such a level of connection with a man until that moment. Uncle-Daddy's words seemed to use my thoughts to formulate his very words. I told him, "I am aware of my actions, and I'm working on it." I assured him that I would take care of it. Uncle-Daddy then said, "That's what I wanted to hear." He and I never discussed smoking again, and I quit smoking cigarettes shortly thereafter, and I haven't smoked another one since!

While en route to my mother's house after dinner, I felt like my wife was up to something. I called her cell phone, but she didn't answer. I called her several more times but only got her outgoing voice mail message.

Finally, my son answered her cell phone, and he couldn't explain to me where his mother was located at the time. In that instance, I knew my wife had taken matters into her own hands and was on her way to my birth mother's home. She wanted to help me by attempting to facilitate a meeting with my birth mother and me after forty-nine years of self-imposed separation. I all but barked at my son to put his mother of the phone, I could not imagine anything good coming from her visit to my birth mother's house only because of the lack of response I had already received from her up to that point, along with the information I had learned from the family members who knew her best.

Once I was able to get my wife on the phone she stated, she was on her way back to my adoptive mother's house and would explain everything when she arrived. All of us arrived at my mother's house at the same time, so my wife's explanation had to wait. I introduced my mother to my maternal uncle, and we sat down together for a small chat.

My mother has always kept a careful eye out for me, and I could tell she was ever so apprehensive about meeting my uncle, as well as about the relationship she could see being forged between us, not because she didn't want this relationship for me but because she was fearful of me being let down by my high expectations of my new relatives, who from her perspective, I didn't know. Eventually, Uncle-Daddy was able to win my mother over, and she partially opened herself up enough to be cordial with him.

Later that evening, my wife and I sat down to discuss the details about why she attempted to confront my birth mother. I asked her, "What compelled you to act on your emotions? Where did you even muster enough courage to knock on her door?" I didn't even have the courage to do that. My wife's response was groundbreaking and provided me with a perspective that I had not previously considered. For the first time, I was asked to view my adoption from a different perspective. As a woman, my wife had a great deal of compassion for my birth mother, and it took me a few minutes to share in her sentiment.

She told me, "I can only imagine the level of hurt and shame your birth mother must have suppressed and locked away for all these years." My wife went on to explain to me that from a psychological perspective many people have an ability to compartmentalize their traumatic experiences. She said that she wanted my birth mother to know that we were good people and we weren't making our advances on her life to criticize or judge her. Unbeknownst to me, earlier in the month following my discovery of the identity of my birth mother, my wife sent her a bouquet of flowers on Mother's Day 2018 with a note attached. My wife had not informed me of her actions or about the message until much later.

A note from my wife to my birth mother on Mother's Day, May 2018:

> Hello, Ms. Harris. My name is Rolonda L. Payne, and I am John Payne's wife. I am sending you this token of my appreciation and acknowledgment for who you are as a woman. I appreciate you for John being here, and I acknowledge that as woman, we make decisions that may not be popular. What has happened is in the past, and I am not here to judge. I am here to say I love you because of who you are as a woman.
>
> Happy Mother's Day!

My Big Brother

Early on Sunday morning, October 28, 2018, I departed Columbia, South Carolina, for Baltimore, Maryland, to ensure I was back in Washington, DC for work on October 29th. During this time, I traveled from my home in South Carolina to Washington, DC for work on a weekly basis. However, this return trip to the Washington Metropolitan Area included a short layover flight in Rochester, New York. Before leaving home, I arranged a meeting with Anthony Lewis, the firstborn child of Sarah which meant he is my big brother. I boarded the plane and settled into my seat for the forty-seven-minute flight. Although the flight time was less than an hour, it seemed much longer maybe because of my overwhelming anticipation of meeting Anthony for the first time. Approximately one week before leaving home, I reached out to my cousin Vanessa to ask if she could suggest a place close to the airport where Anthony and I could meet. I felt that Vanessa more than likely knew of a place because she was raised in Rochester and was quite familiar with the area. From her suggestions, I settled on an Applebee's restaurant just a few miles from the airport, and Anthony agreed to meet me there.

After landing in Rochester, I sent Anthony a text to let him know that I arrived safely. I then proceeded to the ground transportation point to request an Uber ride to Applebee's. When I arrived at the parking lot of Applebee's, I notice the parking lot was empty, and after going into the restaurant, I found that it was empty as well.

I asked the hostess for a table next to a window and followed her to my seat, removed my coat, and sat down. I gazed through the window at the harsh winter weather conditions. Suddenly, a truck pulled into the parking lot, and I thought, this must be the brother I have never met. I watched Anthony exit his truck and walk toward the restaurant's door. After getting a closer look at his face, I knew it was him because of the photos I viewed earlier during my research. As he approached the table, I stood up and reached out to shake his hand. Instead of doing the same, Anthony grabbed my hand and pulled me toward him and hugged me tightly. I couldn't help but feel like a little boy proud to be hugged by his big brother. We sat down and, began talking as if we were raised under the same roof and never lost a day. Due to my level of excitement and the preciousness of the moment, I can't begin to tell you the ins and outs of our conversation, but as far as brothers go, our bond was solidified on that day.

The time seemed to fly and drew closer to the moment I needed to return to the airport for my flight back to Baltimore. I gestured to the waitress and requested the check. When I reached for my wallet, Anthony said, "I'm the big brother, I got this one. You can get the next one!"

For me, the moment was unfamiliar and somewhat unusual; however, I felt good taking the back seat to my big brother. For the first time in my life, I felt like I had someone biological who had my back, not in an emotional way but more of a primitive, physical kind of way. Anthony paid the bill, and we walked outside of the restaurant.

As soon as we were outside, I pulled out my cellphone to request an Uber. Before I could enter the request, Anthony asked, "What are you doing?" I assumed his question was rhetorical, but before I could respond, he said, "Man, get in the truck. You're my brother. I got you!" Without hesitation, I jumped into his truck as instructed. Looking back, I felt like a little boy joyously getting his first opportunity to hang out with his big brother. After arriving at the airport and before we separated, my big brother hugged me again and said, "Man, I'm proud of you!" He also said, "I love you, bro!" In my forty-nine years, I had never heard this combination of words from a biological brother.

Figure 41. John and Anthony meeting in person for the very first time in Rochester, New York, October 28, 2018

Chapter 7

Father's Day 2018

Sunday, June 17, 2018, began with clear Carolina blue skies, warm weather, and my children acknowledging me on Father's Day. Oddly enough, I felt a need to do yardwork, which was weird because it was Sunday and Father's Day, although I've always found doing yardwork extremely therapeutic. While cutting my lawn, the music in my earbuds gave way to constant interuptions by text messages. I stopped for a second to glance at the texts sent by friends and other family members who also wanted to wish me Happy Father's Day. After I finished cutting the lawn, I sat on the porch in my favorite chair to read my text messages in there entirety. One after the other offered kind words of praise about how I've put forth my best effort to be the best father I am capable of being. Instead of basking in their compliments, I became consumed with anger. Only a few short weeks had passed since I met several of my maternal family members, yet I still didn't know my biological father.

Out of desperation, I appealed to several of my maternal family members to hopefully obtain any information they could provide about my adoption that would assist me with locating my biological father. Unfortunately, none of them were able to assist in my cause. So there I sat alone brainstorming all possible angles I could pursue to get the information I desperately needed. I replayed every conversation I previously had with each of my maternal family members and recalled one common thread that ran between each of them. Almost verbatim, every material family member I spoke to said, my birth mother would do anything to protect her reputation!

During this time, I felt so close yet still so far away from achieving my goal of knowing from whom I came. Fed up with my birth mother's lack of response to my attempts to connect with her and her unwillingness to communicate with me made me feel that I needed to change my approach in dealing with her. Instead of continuing to act like the kind son who popped up out of nowhere begging for answers to well-deserved need to know questions, I decided it was time to turn up the heat on my birth mother if I really wanted to find my biological father.

Psychological Warfare

I devised a plan that I was sure she wouldn't like but was certain would provide the effect I was seeking. Although I was sure about my plan, I knew it would certainly damage our already fragile and nonexistent mother-son relationship.

A major component of my plan relied heavily on my birth mother protecting her reputation. I repeatedly rehearsed my plan while accounting for various possibilities that could occur once I set my plan into motion. I was convinced the effects would be equivalent to igniting an explosive in a crowded mall. I briefly thought about the level of desperation I was obviously feeling to stoop to such a level that involved taking the measures I planned to initiate.

The sales experience I received as an army recruiter equipped me with the ability to exploit and take advantage of certain situations and, in some instances, control their outcomes. Already aware that my birth mother wouldn't answer her phone, I decided to call her and patiently wait for her answering machine to pick up. From the information I gathered about her behavior, I learned she screened all calls and wasn't particularly big on using her cell phone.

When her answering machine picked up, I said, "Good afternoon," and then immediately moved into the purpose of my call. I then said, "It's Father's Day and a perfect time for you to reveal the name of my biological father as a Father's Day gift to me." But I already knew she was unwilling to do so. I went on to say, "Through my research, I have obtained the names and addresses of every family member on both sides of your street. I have written a letter that includes photos of the both of us, and I plan to send a copy to each of them, asking if they have any information to offer about my adoption." To place a bow on the box, I closed my voice mail message with, "Not only that, I also plan to send a copy of my letter to the pastor of your church if you don't call me by the end of the day and provide me with the name of my biological father."

After I hung up, not more than a minute had passed when my phone began to ring. I saved my birth mother's number along with a photo of her in my contacts, but it still didn't diminish the shock I felt when I saw her picture on my phone for the very first time in forty-nine years. Due to her supersized ego, my birth mother refers to herself in the third person as Lady Sarah. Knowing that on the other end of the phone was a woman who was highly upset and ready to go to war to protect her reputation, I was armed with the simple knowledge of her name preference.

I thought using it would be the perfect greeting for our first conversation. So I answered the phone and said, "Hello, Lady Sarah!," and our first conversation would be worse than I could have ever imagined! Of course, I expected a war but never believed it would be the equivalent of Armageddon. My birth mother released complete mayhem upon me and all the destructive sounding words she could muster.

Her verbal assault was so intense my only alternative was to just listen. After several minutes of listening to her harsh words about the type of individual she thought I was to threaten to do the things I proposed, the conversation moved swiftly across many topics. To this day, much of what she said only comes to me in bits and pieces. One statement of significance that reverberates with me is her yelling, "You're trying to ruin my life!" She also threatened me by saying, "I'll seek legal counsel and pursue charges against you for harassment!" Not to be outdone, I threw my first verbal jab by offering her a bit of advice, using a piece of information that I was certain only her and I would know. I then said to her, "Getting the legal system involved would not be a wise idea for someone who used a fake name to put her child up for adoption." I went on to say, "I don't believe lying in such a manner would play out well for you in court." Her response to my psychological attack was that of a person who would do anything to protect their reputation, just as most of our closest relatives had revealed. This to me was confirmation that my plan was the best course of action to achieve my objective. Like a snake in waiting, I allowed her to talk until she was out of ammunition. The conversation shifted to a Q and A session.

She began asking me questions that I guess she believed would guilt me out of my desire to know the name of my biological father. She blasted, "I don't know who my birth father is! When I was a young girl, I asked my mother about my father, and she told me she didn't know who he was!" To assassinate my character as a man who simply wanted to trace his roots, she went on to say, "When my mother told me she didn't know who my father was, I just moved on, and I turned out just fine!" Not done, she also said, "I don't understand why you need to know who your father is!"

This statement made me want to know even more. When it was my turn to speak, I was careful with my choice of words, as I was uncertain if I would ever have this opportunity with her again. I said, "I have no intentions of ruining your life. You can make it all go away by simply providing me with the name of my father."

Although I knew it was a lie before it came out, I vowed to my birth mother, that I would honor her desire to remain anonymous and never attempt to contact her again if she would be kind enough to provide me the name of my father.

I Found My Father

After a few minutes, it seemed she was breaking down and, without warning she blurted out, "Your father's name is Ronald Ferguson! He was a police officer, and he was very dear to me! Now go and ruin those people's lives!" I nearly exploded with joy after hearing the name of my father, but I continued to maintain my composure long enough to closeout our call. I steadied my nerves and thanked her for providing me with the best Father's Day gift she could have ever given me, and then I hung up.

I quickly entered the house and walked directly to my desk to begin researching my biological father's name. I knew my birth mother told me the truth because of past research on my second cousin, Curt Parks II. Now the pieces started to snap together like a puzzle, and the connections began to make sense.

Several months earlier, I acquired a copy of my grandfather's (Timothy Ferguson) naturalization papers that listed his sixteen children, and my father was one of them. My grandfather was a first-generation America from Nassau (Forbes

Figure 42. Ronald Ferguson Ocala, Florida, 1960s

Island), Bahamas. With an extreme amount of adrenaline flowing through my body, I discovered articles about my father when he was in high school. He was a standout athlete in baseball, basketball, football, and track & field at Mays High School in Miami, Florida.

After high school, my father attended Mississippi State University for a brief period before enlisting in the U.S. Army. After being honorably discharged from the army, he became a police officer, serving in several cities throughout the state of Florida. Now my imagination really took control over me, and I wondered how it would feel to see my father for the first time—not a mentor, stand-in, or substitute but my real father! Without judgment, I wondered if he knew about me. I caught myself dozing off into a daydream about the both of us sitting together laughing and talking to make up for lost time.

I couldn't reframe from wanting to know what he looked like but couldn't draw an image of him in my mind. In between my daydreaming, I continued my research and what I found next completely broke my heart. My biological father was deceased, and my dream of someday meeting him was forever shattered.

Figure 43. Tim and Mabel Ferguson and daughter Doris

The news of his death left me feeling empty and somewhat exhausted. After discovering my birth mother and her unwillingness to meet me nor form any type of relationship. Everything was now compounded due to the fact I will never get the opportunity to meet my father. I pulled myself up by my bootstraps and forged on knowing that my journey was far from over. I went back to previous research about my paternal grandfather. The whole Bahamas linage really intrigued me and gave me a real since of pride.

I would have been happy just knowing I was from anywhere, but to now know I was the grandson of a direct descendant of a first-generation American who was born and raised in the Bahamas caused my emotions to bubble over with excitement.

After discovering my paternal grandparents, Tim and Mable (Rolle) Ferguson, many events and situations in my past began to make sense all at once. Without reading any academic research, I began to believe and understand that we really do not know ourselves if we do not know our history. Without influence or teachings, there were some small nuances of characterizations that I developed as a child that I could not account for nor explain. As a teenager I would

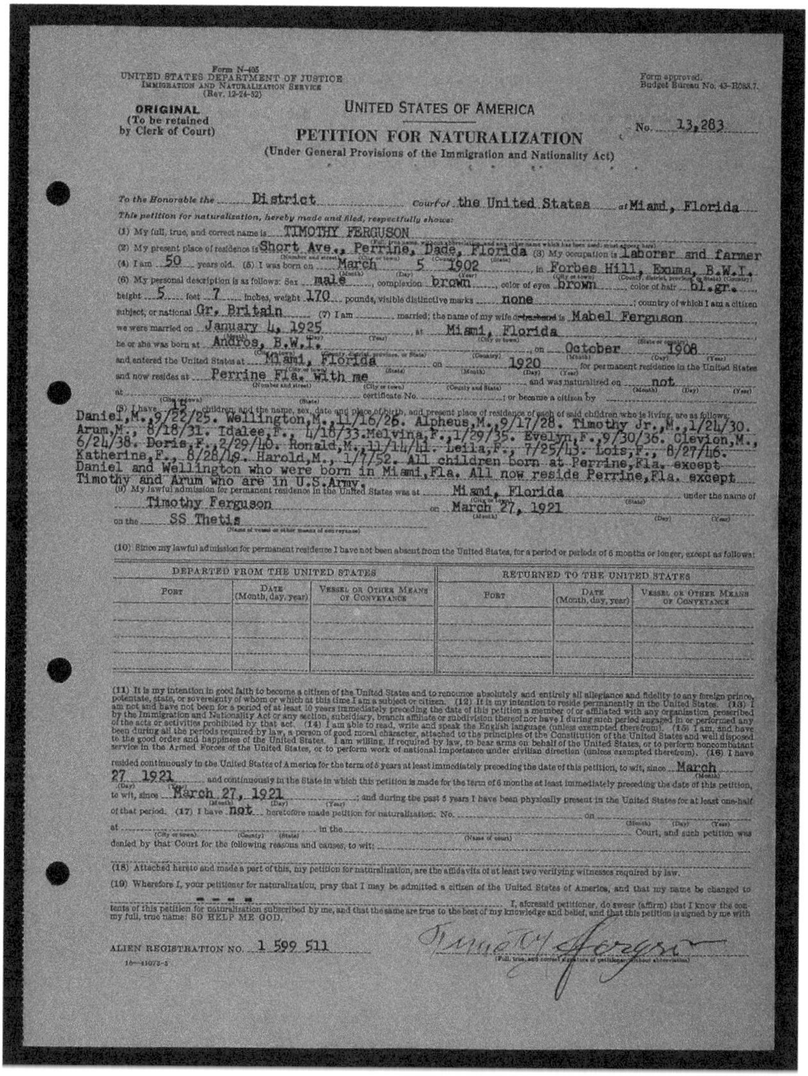

Form N-405
UNITED STATES DEPARTMENT OF JUSTICE
IMMIGRATION AND NATURALIZATION SERVICE
(Rev. 12-24-52)

Form approved.
Budget Bureau No. 43-R088.7.

ORIGINAL
(To be retained by Clerk of Court)

UNITED STATES OF AMERICA

PETITION FOR NATURALIZATION

(Under General Provisions of the Immigration and Nationality Act)

No. 13,283

To the Honorable the District *Court of* the United States *at* Miami, Florida

This petition for naturalization, hereby made and filed, respectfully shows:

(1) My full, true, and correct name is TIMOTHY FERGUSON

(2) My present place of residence is Short Ave., Perrine, Dade, Florida (3) My occupation is laborer and farmer

(4) I am 50 years old. (5) I was born on March 5 1902 in Forbes Hill, Exuma, B.W.I.

(6) My personal description is as follows: Sex male, complexion brown, color of eyes brown, color of hair bl.gr. height 5 feet 7 inches, weight 170 pounds, visible distinctive marks none; country of which I am a citizen subject, or national Gr. Britain (7) I am married; the name of my wife ~~or husband~~ is Mabel Ferguson we were married on January 4, 1925 at Miami, Florida he or she was born at Andros, B.W.I. on October 1908 and entered the United States at Miami, Florida on 1920 for permanent residence in the United States and now resides at Perrine Fla. with me and was naturalized on not at certificate No. ; or became a citizen by

(8) I have 15 children; and the name, sex, date and place of birth, and present place of residence of each of said children who is living, are as follows: Daniel, M., 9/22/25. Wellington, M., 11/16/26. Alpheus, M., 9/17/28. Timothy Jr., M., 1/24/30. Arum, M., 8/18/31. Idalee, F., 4/16/33. Melvina, F., 1/29/35. Evelyn, F., 9/30/36. Clevion, M., 6/24/38. Doris, F., 2/29/40. Ronald, M., 11/14/41. Leila, F., 7/25/43. Lois, F., 8/27/46. Katherine, F., 8/28/49. Harold, M., 1/7/52. All children born at Perrine, Fla. except Daniel and Wellington who were born in Miami, Fla. All now reside Perrine, Fla. except Timothy and Arum who are in U.S. Army.

(9) My lawful admission for permanent residence in the United States was at Miami, Florida under the name of Timothy Ferguson on March 27, 1921 on the SS Thetis

(10) Since my lawful admission for permanent residence I have not been absent from the United States, for a period or periods of 6 months or longer, except as follows:

DEPARTED FROM THE UNITED STATES			RETURNED TO THE UNITED STATES		
PORT	DATE (Month, day, year)	VESSEL OR OTHER MEANS OF CONVEYANCE	PORT	DATE (Month, day, year)	VESSEL OR OTHER MEANS OF CONVEYANCE

(11) It is my intention in good faith to become a citizen of the United States and to renounce absolutely and entirely all allegiance and fidelity to any foreign prince, potentate, state, or sovereignty of whom or which at this time I am a subject or citizen. (12) It is my intention to reside permanently in the United States. (13) I am not and have not been for a period of at least 10 years immediately preceding the date of this petition a member of or affiliated with any organization proscribed by the Immigration and Nationality Act or any section, subsidiary, branch affiliate or subdivision thereof nor have I during such period engaged in or performed any of the acts or activities prohibited by that act. (14) I am able to read, write and speak the English language (unless exempted therefrom). (15) I am, and have been during all the periods required by law, a person of good moral character, attached to the principles of the Constitution of the United States and well disposed to the good order and happiness of the United States. I am willing, if required by law, to bear arms on behalf of the United States, or to perform noncombatant service in the Armed Forces of the United States, or to perform work of national importance under civilian direction (unless exempted therefrom). (16) I have resided continuously in the United States of America for the term of 5 years at least immediately preceding the date of this petition, to wit, since March 27 1921 and continuously in the State in which this petition is made for the term of 6 months at least immediately preceding the date of this petition, to wit, since March 27, 1921; and during the past 5 years I have been physically present in the United States for at least one-half of that period. (17) I have not heretofore made petition for naturalization: No. on at in the Court, and such petition was denied by that Court for the following reasons and causes, to wit:

(18) Attached hereto and made a part of this, my petition for naturalization, are the affidavits of at least two verifying witnesses required by law.

(19) Wherefore I, your petitioner for naturalization, pray that I may be admitted a citizen of the United States of America, and that my name be changed to - - - - I, aforesaid petitioner, do swear (affirm) that I know the contents of this petition for naturalization subscribed by me, and that the same are true to the best of my knowledge and belief, and that this petition is signed by me with my full, true name: SO HELP ME GOD.

ALIEN REGISTRATION NO. 1 599 511

Timothy Ferguson
(Full, true, and correct signature of petitioner without abbreviation)

16—81073-5

Figure 44. Naturalization document of paternal grandfather Timothy Ferguson, March 27, 1921

purposely seek out foods that are indigenous to the Caribbean people long before I obtained my newfound ancestral lineage.

Fried Conch Fritters

After the Gulf War, the army sent me to Fort Riley, Kansas, and it marked my first time in the Midwestern part of the United States. When a person is serving their country as a member of the armed forces, it is the equivalent of legally changing your nationality, at least it can sometimes feel that way. When you are far from home, you tend to gravitate toward others who share common likes or other commonalities such as growing up in the same state.

Shortly after arriving at Fort Riley, I met and befriended Lewis Hill who was another young man from the great state of Florida. Because of his size and stature, everyone who knew him well and considered him a friend called him Big Lew. He and I were in the same unit, and like many young black Floridian males, we were very athletic. On most Saturday mornings, you could find both of us in the gym playing full-court basketball.

Big Lew and I, along with three other guys, would normally dominate the court until we got tired. Many times, after a day of basketball, we met to share a few beers and reminisce about the sunshine state. We conversed about a variety of topics including the weather, fishing, girls, palm trees, and most of all the food. Big Lew was from Miami, and he had a diverse and eclectic palate. He often spoke about eating many Caribbean dishes I had only heard about.

I was raised eating more southern dishes such as collard greens, ham hocks, pig feet, and other dishes passed down from slavery. But Big Lew went on and on about curry and jerk dishes that made you hungry just listening to him. There was one dish he mentioned several times called fried conch fritters. To hide my embarrassment of admitting that I never heard of fried conch or any clue as to what he was talking about, I would just go along with him when he told others that were not from Florida as if I knew what he was talking about. Big Lew finally grew tired of talking about the foods he was accustomed to eating and decided to do something about it. He took a trip to the local grocery store to pick up some conch but quickly learned that you cannot simply walk over to the seafood section of a grocery store in the geographical center of the United States and pick up conch. Big Lew refused to take no for an answer, so the meat supervisor ordered Big Lew some conch and called him when it arrived.

Until the conch arrived, I continued to go along with Big Lew as if I knew what he was talking about and was raised eating Caribbean food too. The day was approaching rapidly, and Big Lew set a date and invited me and others over for what he believed would be a great time of fellowship and good food.

When I arrived at Big Lew's house, I didn't notice anything out of the ordinary for a weekend cookout. There were many familiar faces, and the farmiliar aroma of burning charcoal floated in the air. When Big Lew recognized I was there, he happily greeted me and told me he would be cooking the conch soon and stay close by. Big Lew and I went into the kitchen where I watched him prep the conch before dipping it into the hot grease. When it was done, he prepared both of us a plate, and I carefully watched his every move so I could mimic them, to not let on that I didn't have a clue about what he was doing. Big Lew picked up a lemon wedge and squeezed the juice over the conch, and I quickly did the same. His next move I would have no problems imitating, he took a bottle of hot sauce and vigorously shook it over the conch and so did I. Although I felt as if I was in deep water without apprehension, I picked one up, put it in my mouth, and began chewing. Big Lew was carefully observing me as if he was waiting for my approval. Initially, I thought I would have to fake my way through the situation, but something very unexpected and pleasantly recognizable happened. When the taste of the fried conch hit my taste buds, my brain released a abundance of endorphins. The endorphins interacted with the receptors in my brain and triggered a positive and familiar feeling as if I had been there before. It was like saying hello to an old friend after many years of being apart. It wasn't until some twenty-five years later before I learned why eating fried conch had such an effect on me.

Chapter 8

Genetic Mirroring

After further investigation, I came across additional information about my father. I learned he was once married for several years, and from that union came three girls.

I Have Sisters

Figure 45. Rhonda Rene Ferguson-Lewis

Before my journey began, I had never imagined having a sister and there are not enough words in the *Webster's Dictionary* to adequately express the amount of happiness I felt when I discovered that I have sisters!

Through research, I discovered my biological father was once married, and from that union, three girls were born. Ironically, I discovered them in the order in which they were born, so quite naturally, my research took me down the road of learning about my big sister first. Her name is Rhonda Rene Ferguson-Lewis, my middle sister's name is Rhoda Rejean Ferguson-Carter, and our baby sister is Robin Remona Ferguson-Harvey.

I made every attempt to find as much information as possible about my sisters. They were born in Miami, Florida, and at the time of my discovery lived in the states of Georgia and South Carolina.

To my surprise, my oldest sister lived just seventy-one miles from my home in South Carolina, so I quickly shifted my attention to everything Rhonda! I dove deeper into finding any information the Internet could unveil about her. Then out of nowhere, it happened! I discovered a photo that left no doubt in my mind that Rhonda and I were related. It was the moment I'd waited for ever since becoming familiar with the term genetic mirroring. I yelled downstairs to my wife who I'm sure was already asleep. She rushed upstairs, and I could hardly contain myself enough to explain what I had discovered. My wife gazed at the monitor, and she was just as amazed as I was about the resemblance between the woman on the screen and myself. Immediately, I began drafting a letter to Rhonda to explain my strong inclination about our siblingship. When I was done, I gave the letter a once-over to ensure it was comprehendible and then asked my wife to review it too!

Then came the hard part: I had to decide the method in which I would deliver the letter to Rhonda. Initially, I thought I should mail it as next-day delivery. However, that mode of delivery didn't sit well with me because I suffer from a disease called "lack of patience!" So my next thought was to drive it to the town where she lived and mail it at a nearby post office. I thought, she would receive the letter much faster than if I mailed it from a post office near my house. With care, I inserted the letter into a priority envelope and sealed it. I needed to lie down for a few hours of sleep before setting out on my drive to a post office near Rhonda's house.

The night before my journey, it was difficult for me to fall asleep, but eventually, I dozed off and got a few hours before my alarm clock went off. When it did, I popped out of bed like a jack-in-the-box.

I quickly freshened up, got into my truck, and set the navigation system to an address I obtained through my research. Before getting on the highway, I stopped at the gas station to fuel up and grab a hot cup of coffee.

I didn't waste any time at the pump or getting my much-needed caffeine due to my lack of rim sleep on the night before. Once on the highway, I sank deeply into thoughts of anticipation about what may happen once Rhonda receives my letter. While driving and simultaneously observing the navigation system, I felt there was more road behind me than in front of me to arrive at my destination.

As I got closer, my lack of patience started to kick in again. This time, it was worse than usual, causing me to change my plans. Instead of taking the letter to a post office near her house, I decided to place it directly into her mailbox. After exiting the highway, I drastically reduced my speed to avoid getting a ticket in the small town I had only heard about until this point. As I drove slowly through the town, my lack of patience flared up causing me to change my plans yet again. Instead of placing the letter into her mailbox, I decided that I was going to knock on her door.

My Paternal Angel

I finally arrived at the house of a person who I believed was the firstborn child of Ronald Ferguson. As I slowly pulled into the driveway, I noticed a Florida license plate on a vehicle parked in the driveway.

Seeing a Florida license plate gave more credence to my hypothesis and provided me the courage to exit my truck. With the letter in hand, I slowly walked to the door unsure of what I would say if anyone answered. I cautiously knocked on the door and heard a voice say, "Just a moment!" After a few seconds, the door opened, and it was her, Rhonda! I spent most of the night before staring at her image, absorbing an insane amount of genetic mirroring until I nearly overdosed on anticipation, belief and disbelief, excitement, and amazing hope! Without hesitation, I asked if she was Rhonda Rene Ferguson-Lewis, and she replied, "Yes, I am." I introduced myself and explained why I traveled seventy-one miles to hand deliver a letter to her. I asked Rhonda to call me after she finished reading the letter. Rhonda then asked if I wanted to stay while she read my letter, and I told her that I didn't know if I should stay or not because I had no idea how she may react to the letter. What she did next was more profound than any scene I ever viewed while watching a documentary, weekly series, or movie including the *Antwone Fisher* story I had watched years earlier. She tucked the letter into one of her armpits, stretched both arms toward me with the palms of her hands facing upward, and with authority, she said, "Give me your hands!"

This was not the response I expected, and it caught me completely off guard. Due to my hesitation in complying with her request, she again said, "Give me your hands!" While standing at her front door, I placed my hands in hers and naturally closed my eyes as she began to pray. Remember, I spent all my childhood in church and, therefore, wasn't a stranger to praying, and I could easily tell she wasn't either. However, there was something quite different about her prayer. Each word seemed to penetrate my soul and resonated deep inside my spirit. That moment marked the first time I heard a prayer truly prayed in the past tense as if we met many years earlier and had an established history together. I became completely consumed by my emotions, and eventually, I couldn't maintain my composure any longer. I began to weep as she continued to hold my hands and pray. When Rhonda was done, she told me to come in and have a seat while she read my letter. Rhonda reached into her desk to pull out a pair of glasses and opened the letter to read. Midway through, she looked at me and smiled then went back to reading.

When Rhonda was done, she said something I will never be able to forget. While looking directly into my eyes, she said, "You are, your father's son." To a man who had no inkling of who his father was, Rhonda's words touched me in a way that I have no words to explain. Her words moved me, I felt as if, even though I had never met my father and I didn't know what his voice would sound like or the way he would have said it, but to me, those words were his. She went on to explain that every year during spring break, she volunteers to keep her grandchildren to provide them with an environment that strengthens their family bond. She called one of the oldest of her grandchildren into the room to take a picture of us together. As we posed for our first picture together as siblings, Rhonda kissed me on the cheek, and it was the finishing touch to what will forever be a very special day for me!

Hello Mrs. Rhonda Rene Ferguson-Lewis,

My name is John I. Payne Jr. I was born and adopted August 9, 1969 in Orlando, Florida. My reason for contacting you is because I am of a strong belief that we are related. December of last year I began my journey to find out who my biological parents are and my journey has led me to you. I will try to be as brief as possible but would like to explain how I have come to this conclusion because I want you to have a full understanding of how I got here.

My adopted mother is a wonderful woman and provided me with an outstanding childhood filled with love, patience, and understanding. After graduating from high school, I enlisted in the U.S. Army from where I retired honorable after 20 years of service to our country. I also hold a Bachelor of Science in Business Administration, a Master of Business Administration, and currently pursuing a second Masters degree in Public Administration from the University of Miami. I have never been arrested and I am also a husband of 20 years, a father of three beautiful children. I am currently a Program Analyst in the Federal Government working for the Department of Veterans Affairs in Washington, DC. My purpose for sharing this information is to reassure you that I am in need of nothing but an opportunity to learn more about who I am and from whom I came.

After submitting my DNA to Ancestry.com last December, I received several close relatives matches both from my maternal and paternal side. I was very surprised to find a biological uncle and two brothers, one of which I knew as a child and attended high school with not knowing that we are brothers. After making contact with my uncle it was a matter of time before I was able to put the rest of the pieces together and determine who my biological mother is and that took care of the maternal side. However, my biological mother refused to share with me who my biological father is. I reached out to a 2nd cousin match by the name of Teyana Montgomery from the Miami, Florida area and she shared with me the names of her father and grandmother. Her father's name is Freddy Lee Parks but more importantly her grandmothers name is Ida Lee Ferguson which I am sure you are aware is the sister of Ronald Ferguson. This previous Father's Day, I called my biological mother and was able to convince her to provide me the name of my biological father, and she explained to me that his name is Ronald Ferguson, he is deceased, and was also a police officer for Miami Dade Police Department.

I would like the opportunity to speak with you and share information that may shed some light to this situation, and get answers to so many questions that I have. I can be reached day or night at (███) ███-████ or by email at ████████████.com at your convenience.

Figure 46. A letter John wrote to who he believed is Ronald Ferguson's first born child and his big sister, Rhonda Rene Ferguson-Lewis

Figure 47. John's first kiss from his sister Rhonda.

Rhonda and I sat on her front porch and talked for hours as if we had known each other all our lives. Somewhere in the conversation, I asked if she would be willing to submit to a DNA test, and she laughed. After a brief chuckle, she finally said, "Listen, you're my brother, no doubt about it. But I know you want the scientific evidence. So bring your little DNA kit over here, and we will put the stamp on it!"

After what seemed like a very long time, I gave her a hug and kissed her on the cheek. I got into my truck for the seventy-one-mile drive home. Once I was out of town and away from traffic lights, I called my wife to share the good news. The next morning, I jumped out of the bed like a U.S. Army private undergoing basic training. I thought, this was too much to digest alone and I needed someone else to share in my experience. After a few seconds, I decided to share this momentous occasion with my oldest son. Without letting the cat out of the bag, I got him up, and we drove back to Rhonda's house so he could experience the discovery of our paternal side of the family for himself. Once again, I pulled into her driveway, just as I had done on the day before. After exiting my truck, I asked my son to knock on the door because I wanted to observe his expression when he laid eyes on his aunt for the first time.

He knocked on the door, and she opened it. My oldest son stood there in amazement, repeatedly saying, "Daddy, you two look just alike!" I introduced my son to his aunt, and we went inside and sat down. After a few minutes of conversation, we went through the process of collecting her saliva sample.

When Rhonda was done, she sealed the tub and placed it inside the collection bag which was then placed into the return mailer and sealed. After a brief second, Rhonda held the DNA kit high above her head and said, "To a siblingship that was created in heaven and manifested on earth." She turned to me, and while handing me the sealed kit, she said, "Here, little brother, go get your peace!" After leaving her house, I made a beeline to the nearest post office, but I couldn't stop thinking about what she said before handing me the return mailer. Rhonda was exactly right. If the results returned positive, it would bring me some amount of peace.

Waiting for the results seemed like years, and while we waited, Rhonda shared information about our other siblings with me to tide me over until the DNA result was posted on my Ancestry account. We discussed meeting my other two siblings, but I insisted we wait on the scientific evidence just to cover any doubts.

Robin Remona Ferguson-Harvey

In the meantime, Rhonda and I shared contact information, and my youngest sister Robin was the next of my sisters that I got the opportunity to speak with over the phone. I saved her number and a photograph that I copied from the Internet to my contacts.

One morning after getting my first cup of coffee, my phone rang, and my sister's picture appeared. We made quick work of the pleasantries by providing information about our children and a little about our childhoods.

Figure 48. John with his sister Robin Remona Ferguson-Harvey, August 12, 2018

I can still remember the accepting, inviting, and pleasant conversation we had. Robin explained while growing up, she always wanted a brother, and that tidbit of information left me feeling high on life the entire day because it meant both of us were open to the idea of a siblingship.

By calling me before I called her, Robin broke the ice between us; and thereafter, it was easier for me to pick up the phone and call her simply to hear her voice. After we talked, I could hardly contain myself and thought, *I have sisters!*

Rhoda Rejean Ferguson-Carter

Rhoda is my middle sister, and according to Rhonda, she would not come easily. Apparently, despite being married to their mother, our father was a bit of a lady's man and fathered several children outside of the marriage, which explained the two additional children listed in his obituary.

As twisted as this may sound, the two illegitimate children sup-ported Rhonda's earlier statement that our father didn't make a habit out of disowning any of his children.

This gave weight to the possibility that he was unaware of my birth, which brought relief to me in a strange sort of way. Now knowing I have three sisters, my goal was to develop a relationship with each of them. I came to realize that there was something inside me that belonged to each of them collectively and individually, as well as each of them held something within them that was special and just for me! I tried to put myself in Rhoda's shoes and imagined how she must have felt learning once again; there was yet another person claiming to be a child of her father. At the outset of my journey, I knew this situation could exist, and I thought about the ways I would deal with it.

Figure 49. Rhoda Rejean Ferguson-Carter

First, I knew it was important for Rhonda's DNA result to be returned before I made any attempts to physically connect with the rest of the family. While waiting on her DNA result, I thought it was important for me to keep the momentum going, consider-ing the communication established with two out of three sisters I later came to call my trifecta, so I wrote my middle sister, Rhoda, a letter.

After Rhoda received my letter, her next move was vintage John Payne. If there was any doubt in my mind, it was instantly removed after our first conversation. She called me to bring clarity to her posi-tion and feelings about my discovery.

I knew without a shadow of a doubt that this was the branch of the tree I belonged to and originated from. Her words were my words, and given the information and circumstances, I would have responded in the same fashion as she did. Rhoda confirmed much of what our big sister, Rhonda, shared with me about several people claiming space on an already crowded family tree. Although this was not a conversation filled with joy and anticipation of connecting, I was left with a lot of information to work with. From our conversation, I knew exactly who Rhoda was and given the proper space and time we would someday grow to love each other as siblings. Among a few nicknames I gave her is Pop Tart, which will forever be my description of such an understanding and wonderful but cautious woman.

Rhoda is a female given name, originated in both Greek and Latin. Its primary meaning is "rose" but it can also mean "from Rhodes", the Greek Island originally named for its roses. The name was mostly used in the 18th and 19th centuries but goes back at least to the first century as it is recorded in the New Testament of the Bible.

My dear sister (and I say that with the upmost of respect),

The passage above is the meaning of your name and my reason for starting this letter in this Fashion is to not overlook that every rose has her thorns. I would like to express to you that I understand how you must feel. I worked tirelessly with many sleepless nights to find you! Your perspective and feelings about our father and some of the mistakes he may have made are all valid however, it is important to me that you know I have loved and longed for you long before I knew you existed! I had no idea of what or whom I would find when I started this journey, and had no expectations going into this; I could not even wrap my mind around the fact that I would have had siblings but I am extremely happy that I found you!

I am asking that you allow me the opportunity to get to know you exactly where you are in this unexpected and awkward occasion for the both of us. Although our father may not have made the best decisions when it came to children outside of what was supposed to be a sacred union between him and your mother, there is some good that can come of all of this. I am coming to you humbled from the many things life has thrown at me and I have seen it ALL! But through it all I have managed to persevere and make the best of every situation.

In closing, I only ask of you one favor! Please grant me the opportunity to develop (at your pace) a genuine and meaningful sibling relationship, and that you not hold me responsible for the sins of our father. Once I knew of your existence, I can't think of nothing else but meeting you and your wonderful Family, and to also be in your presence. I want for nothing, and need for nothing "but to know you!"

Fortunate to be your brother,

John Isham Payne Jr.

Figure 50. Letter from John to his sister Rhoda, 2018

I could only imagine how Rhoda felt when she heard my nickname for her, but it bears no negative connotation. Rhoda has a slightly hard exoskeleton with a soft inside that if you are fortunate enough to get to know her, she is the most caring and loving person you could ever meet. However, just like me, you don't want to be on the receiving end of her wrath.

The Trifecta

Figure 51. John with his sisters from (l to r) Robin, Rhonda, and Rhoda, August 2018

The day finally arrived, Rhonda's DNA result posted on my Ancestry account, and to no surprise, she was scientifically proven to be my sister. The firstborn child of Ronald Ferguson and I shared enough DNA to supersede all other connections identified by Ancestry before her sample was processed. Although this was no surprise, it validated my existence and place in the world and proved that Rhonda is, in fact, my big sister and Ronald Ferguson is my father. Excited, I immediately called Rhonda to let her know that I wanted to meet the rest of my family!

Without any hesitation, Rhonda spearheaded the efforts to gather the family, Rhoda reserved the restaurant where we would meet, and Robin recommended a lodging location for my family and I to stay while in town.

The morning of August 7, 2018, was a few days short of my forty-ninth birthday, my wife and I headed south to Albany, Georgia, while Rhonda and her husband also departed South Carolina for the same destination. After arriving and settling into our hotel for the night, I awoke early in anticipation of meeting my Ferguson siblings, along with nieces and nephews I didn't previously knew I had. After coffee, I typed the address of the restaurant into my navigation system and headed to the location.

I arrived, parked, and sat in the parking lot to see if I could recognize anyone going into the restaurant mainly because I was extremely nervous. After all, it's not every day that a forty-eight-year-, eleven-month-, and twenty-eight-day-year-old-man meets his biological family for the first time. As my family and I sat in the truck staking out the front door of the restaurant, I noticed Rhoda exiting her car. Like a deer caught in headlights, I just sat there, frozen in time with no clue of what to do. I intensely watched her walk across the parking lot and into the restaurant before I could gather enough nerves to get out of my truck.

My family and I entered the restaurant, just as Rhoda had done a few minutes before. The unusual thing about the entire event is that I recognized them all right away as if I had seen them before and my nervousness disappeared just as fast as it had come; I felt like it was where I belonged. My family and I walked into the reserved room, and that signaled the start of the event. I can't remember the first few minutes, but I can recall the warmness of the atmosphere I felt while in the presence of my people. I have always been a person to attack my issues straight on and never from an angle. So I purposely sat next to Rhoda to take advantage of the opportunity to get to know her better and maybe gain her approval.

Like a force to be reckoned with, she stood up from the table and began to speak. My sisters presented me with gifts and kind words that welcomed me into the family.

This was my Antoine Fisher moment, and I can't tell you how good it felt to be accepted as a member of the Ferguson family. My youngest sister gave me a Hallmark card, and I knew that much thought had gone into her selection.

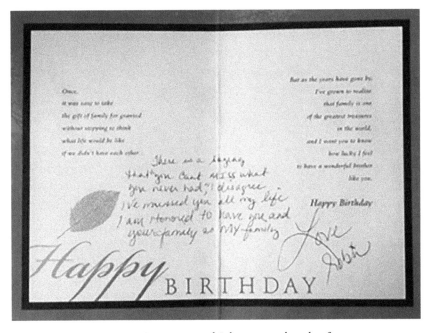

Figure 52. Greetings card John received on his forty-ninth birthday from his sister Robin, 2018

Before meeting my sisters, my wife and I had planned a special event for my sisters and I to celebrate our siblingship. I couldn't wait to show my appreciation and gratitude. I took my sisters on a spa date to spend a relaxing and soothing day together. As we sat in the massage chairs receiving pedicures, they began to sing. The three of them sang their rendition of the song "We Are Family" from the 2006 movie *Dreamgirls*.

Everyone in the salon, including myself, was amazed, and when they were done, the entire salon applauded their perfect harmony. As for me, I was high on cloud nine!

Figure 53. Siblings at the spa from (l to r) Rhonda,
Rhoda, John, and Robin, August 2018

I returned to my hotel room to get some rest from the day's festivities and received a call from my sisters asking me to meet them in the lobby. For the sake of brevity due to my level of excitement, I avoided using the elevator and walked down the stairs to the lobby.

When I arrived to the landing overlooking the lobby, I saw my sisters waiting at a table in the middle of the dining area. My level of excitement for having an opportunity to interact with my brand-new sisters caused me to have temporary tunnel vision. When I got closer to them, I noticed a cake and a few gifts on the table. My sisters threw me a birthday party in a small intimate space that quickly became one of my top moments ever in life. When I sat down at the table, they began singing Stevie Wonder's rendition of "Happy Birthday" before lighting the candles on the cake.

After I blew the candles out one of my sisters sliced the cake, my wife and I sat with the three of my sisters laughing and talking for hours. It was as if we never missed a day!

Figure 54. John celebrating his forty-ninth birthday with his
wife, children, and sisters in Albany, Georgia, August 2018

Momma Turns Eighty

After returning home from fellowshipping with my sisters, Robin called and gave me the greatest compliment I have every received. I still blush every time I think about it! She told me I was perfect in every way and that she wanted to meet the woman who raised me. My wife and I planned a birthday dinner to celebrate my mother's eightieth birthday, and we invited my sisters to help us celebrate the woman credited for raising me. During my earlier call with Robin, I told her that my mother and I were born in August and that our birthdays were only four days apart.

My family and I made a quick turnaround on our trip from Georgia to South Carolina in order to make it to Florida in time for the surprise birthday dinner. After arriving in Florida, I quickly developed a PowerPoint presentation to provide my mother with an update on my genealogy search. I reviewed my presentation to ensure that I covered the information that was most important, saving the information about my sisters for the end.

This would allow my mother to retain the names and associations before introducing them later in the evening. Before leaving for the restaurant, I sat down at the dining room table with my mom and step-father to share my presentation.

When I was done, I answered their questions before we headed out for what I was sure would be a great birthday celebration. My wife sent me a text to provide information I needed to maintain the element of surprise. When we arrived, I escorted my mother into the restaurant, and when we reached the door of the room my wife reserved, everyone inside yelled, "Surprise!" My mother's face lit up like New York City's Time Square. She became overwhelmed with emotion when she saw everyone's face that came to surprise her. One of my mother's sisters who still resides in her hometown of Opelika, Alabama, was there, along with several members of my mother's church.

As we made our way around the room, my mother whispered into my ear and asked, "Are those your sisters?" She couldn't believe that my biological sisters wanted to meet her and traveled from

Georgia to help celebrate her birthday. Like my precious mother, I was overwhelmed with emotion as I watched the woman that raised me and had given me every ounce of her love for over forty years interacted with my biological sisters whom I had only met one week prior. Everything was as it was meant to be!

Figure 55. Sisters Robin (l), and Rhoda (r), at the eightieth birthday celebration of John's mother Ada M. Hightower (center), August 12, 2018

Uncle Clevion

After dinner with my maternal family and before meeting my birth mother, I turned my attention to more research on my paternal family. With very little effort, I discovered my father had a living brother named Clevion Ferguson who I later learned went by the name Cleveland due to a mix-up in the spelling of his name when he enlisted in the army over sixty years earlier.

Uncle Cleveland was located about an hour's drive from my home, and I felt it was important to meet him. I quickly jotted down his contact information and rehearsed what I would say when I called. After meeting my sisters and other relatives on my paternal

Figure 56. John meeting his uncle Clevion Ferguson, St. George, South Carolina, September 5, 2018

side of the family, I felt more empowered than ever as I dialed his number. Everything I rehearsed went up in smoke when his wife answered the phone. My biggest mistake was announcing myself as Uncle Cleveland's nephew as if they already knew me. This was largely due to the confidence I gained by meeting other members of my paternal family. My new-found aunt asked, "Why haven't I heard of you?" I explained that I was adopted and shared with her my personal journey to find my biological family members which guided me to the moment we were sharing.

For the first time in my life, I had enough knowledge about my bloodline to be able to name-drop—primarily my sisters' names—on other family members during my cold calls to them.

After mentioning my father's name, I drop the names of my trifecta, my sisters. At the beginning of our conversation, my aunt informed me that my uncle was unavailable; however, as I was completing the story about my journey, Uncle Cleveland walked through the door. My aunt asked me to hold on, and I could hear her tell Uncle Cleveland that he had a call. He asked his wife, "Who is it?"

She replied, "He'll tell you!"

When he got on the phone, we didn't waste any time getting to the point. I explained to him how I arrived at the point of calling him, and when he felt he had enough information, he said,

"Well then, we need to meet." Uncle Cleveland gave me his address which matched the information I found during my research. We confirmed the details of our meeting, and not long thereafter, we ended our call.

Early the next morning, I was on the road to connect with another newfound relative. I found myself driving down a long country South Carolina road with a field of cotton on my left and a heavy wooded area on my right until I pulled into my uncle's driveway. As I was exiting my truck, he was simultaneously walking out of his front door headed in my direction. When he got closer, he asked, "Young man, how tall are you?"

I answered, "I'm six feet and one inch tall, Sir!"

His response was very enlightening and empowering to my confidence, although I was already aware that I would never meet my father. Uncle Cleveland said, "That was the exact height your father was!"

Uncle Cleveland explained that he was eighty years old and in a subtle way provided a good report concerning his mental health before saying at that very moment he felt like he was with his brother again while in my presence. We walked into the house, sat, and talked for a while about my father and his childhood. Unannounced, he grabbed a folder and stack of what appeared to be documents and pictures. Uncle Cleveland explained that he had been in possession of the documents for more than thirty years since the passing of my father.

While looking somewhat puzzled, Uncle Cleveland revealed to me that he was unsure as to why he chose to hang on to my father's items. Then he said, "Here, nephew, these belong to you."

As he was leading up to this moment, I already knew where he was going, and I couldn't contain my emotions. As if someone poured coffee into my cup until it ran over and spilled onto the saucer beneath it, we found ourselves hugging and crying together, in the middle of his livingroom floor.

Veterans Day 2018

Figure 57. Clevion Ferguson military photo

Uncle Cleveland and I shared information about each other and the many places life had taken us. I learned my uncle had fought in the Korean War, and we spent time swapping our war stories. A few days after meeting, I gave him a call about two week before Veterans Day. During our conversation, I informed my uncle that I would be in town on Veterans Day and would like to take him to breakfast. He accepted my invitation, and we ended our phone call. The week leading up to Veterans Day, my uncle and I did not speak, but it did not damper my excitement of celebrating the holiday with my father's brother.

Veterans Day came, and I woke early to make the hour drive to my uncle's home in South Carolina. My adrenaline was high as I got closer to picking up uncle Cleveland to share in what I feel is a great day for all Veterans. I arrived at my uncle's home at 7:30 a.m. on Veterans Day, and before I could exit the vehicle, my uncle was walking out his door ready to go and partake in the Veterans Day breakfast we were to share together. I asked my uncle, "How did you know I would be here so early?"

And my uncle replied, "Because you are a Ferguson!"

November 12, 2018, will go down in history as one of the best Veterans Day I have ever observed!

A few weeks after meeting my father's brother, he traveled from South Carolina to Miami, Florida, to attend the first service of one of

Figure 58. John (l), and Cleveland Ferguson Veterans Day, November 12, 2018

his sons at a new church where he was named senior pastor. Due to his age, as he made his way down I-95 south, Uncle Cleveland stopped at relative's homes to provide his family and himself breaks from the rigors of travel. Not only did he take breaks from his travel, he also took the time to spread the word about me to my paternal cousins. Armed only with a picture of me, he told any family member who would listen about the lost son of his deceased brother, Ronald Ferguson.

A Cousin Name Peaches

When Uncle Cleveland made it to Miami, he called to inform me he had made it safely. I was extremely impressed because I have never seen an eighty-year-old man move about the earth in the way he does.

I thought, his youthfulness at eighty might be a blessing in disguise reserved for my later years. No longer than a few minutes after we ended our call, I received a call from Sandra Parks, a first cousin who lives in Jacksonville, Florida. She talked about the conversation Uncle Cleveland and she had and wanted to meet me right away. I was thrilled that a cousin whom I had never met was excited about meeting me! My wife and I have been married for over twenty years, and our entire marriage has been limited of family on my side.

Figure 59. Sandra (Peaches) Parks

So I wanted to proceed with caution because I didn't want to cause any damage to my marriage, given that most of my time was normally dedicated to my immediate family with no competing factors other than periodic visits to spend time with my mother. Because of the rapid pace in which I was discovering my kinfolks, I needed to find balance between my discoveries and my immediate family. A week later, Peaches called me and asked when I was coming to see her. She felt my timeline was not working well for her. So Peaches offered to pay for my flight to get a chance for us to

Figure 60. John and his cousin Peaches

bond and for me to meet even more paternal family members. My wife and I discussed the trip to Jacksonville and then contacted my cousin, Vanessa, to ask if she would watch our children while we journeyed to Florida. After Vanessa agreed, we scheduled our flight for the next weekend. Knowing Albany, Georgia, was not far from Jacksonville, I decided to give my sisters a call to ask if they would join me at our cousin's house. I thought it was a good idea for them to accompany me because many years had passed since they took the opportunity to spend time with our Ferguson relatives.

My cousin Peaches opened her home and her heart, and from our first in-person meeting, I felt as comfortable as being in my own home. She hosted a family cookout and two of my sisters along with other relatives welcomed me into the family.

Figure 61. Ferguson Family Crest

Chapter 9

The Perfect Movement of God

Uncle-Daddy, who is never short of time to provide me a healthy dose of mental stimulation, offered a thought-provoking discussion on biblical numerology during one of our many phone calls. He asked if I was familiar with the topic, and I told him that I didn't know anything about it. He began discussing the number 9 and a few insightful meanings about the number which is used several times in scripture. It is a symbol of divine planning, finality, and full cycle. For example, Christ died in the ninth hour (3:00 p.m.), Yom Kippur—the Day of Atonement—occurs at sunset on day 9 of the seventh Hebrew month (Lev. 23:32), the fruit of the Spirit consist of nine qualities (love, joy, peace, patience, goodness, kindness, gentleness, faithfulness, and self-control [Gal. 5:22]). Other than an occasional purchase of a lottery ticket, I have never given any thought to the role numbers play in the lives of people, especially mine. However, after talking with Uncle-Daddy, I took a deeper look at the role number 9 has played in my life. One meaning that resonated with me is the number 9 described as the perfect movement of God.

While still in my birth mother's womb, God's perfect movement was in full operation over my life. For example, I was born August 9, 1969, and in 2003, I asked my mother for her blessings to search for my biological mother, and because of her mind-set at the time, she refused. Fifteen years later and out of nowhere, my mother called to give her blessings for me to "find my people." The significance of this timing is if she had given me her blessings in 2003, I am certain that I wouldn't have had as much success, if any, finding my biological bloodline, and more than likely would have given up because it would have been too difficult without DNA testing.

When I became aware that my paternal sister Rhonda lived only seventy-one miles from me, she became the angel that welcomed me into the Ferguson family, as well as presented me to the rest of my paternal siblings. When I connected with Uncle-Daddy, we shared so much in common, and are members of the same fraternity which, I am certain was very instrumental in the development of our relationship. Like Rhonda, Uncle-Daddy allowed God to use him as the instrument that reintroduced me to my birth mother. He is also responsible for sharing knowledge of me with the rest of my maternal family members.

Corey and I attended the same high school and knew each other as classmates; this information proved helpful as I started to close in on the identity of my birth mother.

My Fiftieth Birthday

After finding and meeting with my paternal sisters, my journey felt like an emotional roller coaster. While reflecting on the year before when for the first time I was with my sisters celebrating my forty-ninth birthday. The amount of family I discovered was overwhelming for me, considering the year before I was totally unaware of my biological family.

My wife and I talked about what a fiftieth birthday party would look like for me and who I might invite. I rattled off a few names, and by the time I was finished, my list grew to nearly one hundred people. I have always been a lover of people, and over the years, I have acquired lots of acquaintances and friends probably because I was raised as an only child. Looking back at my list, it appeared my life was well spent, rich in friendships and love. In addition to my acquaintances and friends, I added my biological relatives because I was sure they would make my birthday party even more memorable.

After much thought, I told my wife that I wanted to celebrate my birthday at home rather than a location somewhere in a distant place, and she agreed. My wife then contacted my cousin Vanessa to help her plan the party. The day of my party finally arrived, and the weather was sunny and warm. I sat in my upstairs bedroom as the first few acquaintances, biological family members, coworkers, fraternity brothers, and friends arrived. As the noise level and number of guests increased, I decided it was time to walk downstairs to greet and mingle with my guests. At one point, I looked down onto the patio from the above deck and witnessed my relatives engaging in conversation and laughter with my friends. I stood there watching for a few minutes to embrace the moment; everything was just as I had hoped. Anthony was talking to one of my coworkers, Rhoda was sitting in my home theater and talking with the wives of my friends, and Gus was mingling with my paternal cousins from Florida. As I walked around, it occurred to me that family and friends had traveled from Albany, Georgia; Birmingham, Alabama; Charlotte, North Carolina; Columbia, South Carolina; Houston, Texas; Jacksonville and Miami, Florida, who thought enough of me to travel to Maryland to help me celebrate my fiftieth birthday.

My house was transformed into a place suitable for celebrating the birthday of a king. The main level was decorated in the party's theme "Forever Young," which was a throwback from the 1980s.

Accompanying the decorations was an extended table topped with a wide variety of food for everyone to enjoy. To make the day even more special than it already was, Rhoda pulled me aside to share a special sibling moment and presented me with gifts. To many, this may have little significance, but to me, it marked only the second time in fifty years that I shared my birthday with a sibling. Just when I thought things

Figure 62. John and his niece Cynthia Hartman

couldn't get any better, Anthony invited his daughter to meet me for the first time, as well as join in the festivities.

Cynthia, my niece, and daughter of my oldest maternal brother played a vital role in finding my biological bloodline, and I was overjoyed about the opportunity to meet her in person.

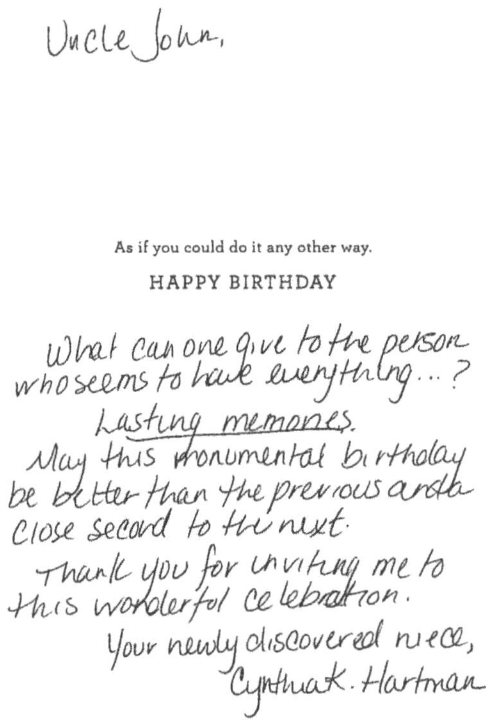

Uncle John,

As if you could do it any other way.

HAPPY BIRTHDAY

What can one give to the person who seems to have everything...?
Lasting memories.
May this monumental birthday be better than the previous and a close second to the next.
Thank you for inviting me to this wonderful celebration.
Your newly discovered niece,
Cynthia K. Hartman

Figure 63. Greeting card from Cynthia to her uncle John Payne, August 2019

I wanted to thank her for her contribution to my success because it was her idea and encouragement that caused Anthony to submit his DNA for testing. Without either of them knowing, I had already submitted my DNA for testing. It was the DNA match of Anthony and I that essentially connected the puzzle pieces in my journey to find my biological mother. His DNA was my first close relative match and accounts for the discovery of my entire maternal bloodline. Cynthia came by the house the day before my birthday party, and when we met face-to-face, we instantly connected. Like me, she was also full of questions. We talked for what felt like hours. I provided Cynthia with as much information about our bloodline as I possibly could. She returned on the day of my party and presented me with a framed picture of us that was taken when we met the day before and a birthday card that was filled with sincere words, which were an honest and heartfelt interpretation of me, given it was our first time ever meeting each other. "I have traveled to many places in the world for birthdays and vacations. However, my fiftieth birthday party was by far the best celebration I have ever had!"

Figure 64. John Payne's biological family members photo taken August 10, 2019, at his fiftieth birthday celebration in Fort Washington, Maryland

58:26

Approximately one month and eighteen days after my fiftieth birthday, I got the opportunity to do the impossible: I met my birth mother again, since birth. About two years before our scheduled meeting, I began my search for her with a gaping hole in my heart, a strong need to know where I came from and from whom, and a false name of my birth mother.

In early September 2019, Uncle-Daddy called me after a conversation with his sister who is also my birth mother. He told me that he brokered a meeting between her and I. Uncle-Daddy asked me when I could travel to Orlando so he could put the finishing touches on the masterpiece God had allowed him to mediate. Amazingly enough, my wife had already arranged my travel to Orlando for September 27 to conduct my quarterly health and welfare check on my mother and stepfather, so I told Uncle-Daddy that I was already scheduled to be in Orlando. He said, "Great," and mentioned that it was important for us to strike while the iron was hot so as to not allow any room for my birth mother to renege on her promise to meet with me. Uncle-Daddy called later that day to tell me that she agreed to meet at 1:00 p.m., September 27, 2019.

The morning that would bring me full circle in my initial purpose for setting out on my genealogical journey finally arrived. I awoke early in anticipation of what the day might bring. My sister Robin drove from Georgia to Florida to lend her moral support. She waited with my mother and stepfather in their home for the outcome of my meeting with my birth mother. Uncle-Daddy and I spoke on several occasions about what time to pick me up from my mother's house so we would arrive at my birth mother's on time. I found it difficult to determine a departure time because of the close proximity of my mother and birth mother. This may be hard to believe, but for the majority of my childhood, my mother and birth mother live only 3.1 miles apart.

Before Uncle-Daddy arrived, my mother shared with me that she had reconnected with her old friend, Josephine, who was my delivery nurse and she agreed to meet with me as well. My mother said Josephine was excited about seeing me again; after all, she hadn't laid eyes on me since the day I was born. Knowing there would be a host of people waiting on the outcome of my first meeting with my birth mother as an adult, I suggested that afterwards, we meet at a local restaurant where I would fill them in on what took two years and a life-time to come to fruition.

Uncle-Daddy arrived, and I gave my mother a kiss and thanked her for giving her blessings to find my biological mother. I hugged my sister Robin and thanked her for her much-needed moral support and unwavering love. Uncle-Daddy and I departed for my birth mother's house, and while en route, he called to let her know we were on the way. When she answered the phone, he told her that we would arrive earlier than scheduled, she then said, she was ready and expecting our arrival.

We pulled into her driveway, and before exiting the car, Uncle-Daddy asked, "Nephew, are you ready?"

I responded, "No," as we both were opening our doors and sliding out of the car. I allowed him to lead the way to her front door. Uncle-Daddy rang the doorbell, and shortly thereafter, it opened. There stood the initial reason I began my search, the woman who gave birth to me, and the cause for many hours of research.

She stood in the opened door with an air of not having a care in the world. Uncle-Daddy reintroduced us by saying, "Sarah, this is your son, John Isham Payne, Jr. Nephew, this is your mother, Sarah Lee Harris-Fallings." And then everything became extremely awkward. My birth mother seemed caught off guard and turned to Uncle-Daddy before refocusing her attention on me and said, "I was unaware this was going to happen today, but since you're here, I guess we can get this over with!" I found her actions and words very odd because I was present when Uncle-Daddy called her just a few minutes prior to us arriving.

Uncle-Daddy had provided me with a warning about the possibility of my birth mother suffering from early onset dementia some days earlier. We stood at the front door for a few more awkward seconds while Uncle-Daddy reminded her of the purpose of our visit and then she invited us inside. After entering her house for the first time, I reflected on how close she lived to where I grew up.

As I observed my surroundings, I thought about my brother Corey, now sitting in the house where he lived while growing up as well as my birth mother was here all the while, hiding in plain sight. As I gazed at the walls and imagined that at one time they might have been decorated with Corey's pictures and achievements, I also thought of the mutual classmates of Corey and I who might have visited both of us during the same time frame but at different locations not knowing that we are brothers. Months before our meeting, I recalled a conversation with my big brother Anthony, and he described to me what the inside of our mother's house looked like based on his memory from the last time he was granted permission to visit. Anthony recalled pictures of Corey being the only ones hung on the walls and how it made him feel to not be represented on the walls of our birth mother's house.

I tried, as much as I could, to look around without seeming to conspicuous, but I didn't see any pictures of Anthony or Corey hanging on the walls. I chuckled to myself, thinking I bet she didn't have a picture of me anywhere around here either.

Our meeting was slow getting started with most of our initial discussion involving me attempting to set my birth mother at ease by letting her know that I was not there to cast judgment. I explained to her that I was only seeking answers to questions that would provide me with a perspective on my life and purpose. After a few minutes, I felt as if I was rambling because I only had a short time to unpack fifty years of emotional curiosity. In my head, I created a list of questions and like an Excel spreadsheet I conducted a mental filter to prioritize them from greater to least in importance. My years of training as an army recruiter taught me how to blend questions into casual conversation, and I was waiting for the right moment to utilize my questioning technique. For this to work, I would have to quickly establish rapport with my birth mother. However, just as I was about to start my inconspicuous line of conversational questioning, my birth mother made a statement that sucked the wind out of my sail leaving me mentally stranded in the middle of my thoughts.

Her statement instantly made it difficult for me to breathe as if I was unexpectedly punched in the stomach, rendering my diaphragm momentarily inoperable. Before making her statement, she talked about not wanting to come across as cruel. Although I wish our first encounter would have gone better, the truth is, I met a stranger who did not have the capacity to love me or her other two sons again.

The reason I use the word *again* is because she must have loved me once before, she carried me for nine months and allowed me a chance at life, knowing she had other less desirable options. After our conversation about her not wanting to be viewed as cruel, she said, "I hope this brings you peace, because I was at peace when I gave you up!" Her words hit me like a twenty-pound sledgehammer, and her indifferent demeanor instantly hardened me. I sat looking her directly in the face and said to myself, "If she was at peace with this, well, so am I!" Suddenly, the questions I wanted answered eluded me. Somehow, they were no longer important to me, and I chalked it up as "mission complete." A little over one year before our reintroduction. I began my search with a desire to find my birth mother, a false maternal name, and a birth certificate that was certified seven years after my date of birth.

With a broken heart, I tried one last time to see if there was anything left for me inside this woman. I informed my birth mother that I cannot explain it, but I needed her to know that I love her. She looked at me and said, "I don't understand that." Her response caused Uncle-Daddy who had maintained his silence the entire time to speak out. He asked his sister, "How can you say you love God but you can't love the man sitting next to you—in this case, the son you gave birth to?" By then, I had mentally checked out. I tried to fill the additional time with light conversation that had little relevance to anything. After vacantly looking around the room, my birth mother offered me a tour of her home and shared some of her arts and crafts with me. They occupied the time she spent at home, alone and oblivious to caring and feelings. I finally told Uncle-Daddy I was ready to leave, and the three of us moved to the front door.

I didn't want to burn the start of what could someday become a bridge, so I told my birth mother that I am available should she ever wanted to reach out to talk and with a empty hug our encounter was over. I am extremely doubtful that my birth mother and I will ever communicate on a meaningful level or that she will ever show me the type of love and respect that I hoped for.

However, I had accomplished what I set out to do, and for that, I will be forever grateful!

Dinner with Ms. Josephine

Figure 65. Dinner with from (l to r) Ada Hightower (Mom), John Hightower (Pop), John Payne, Eddie Harris (Uncle-Daddy), Robin Ferguson-Harvey (Sister), and Josephine Peterson (John's delivery nurse), September 27, 2019

As planned, Uncle-Daddy and I met my mother, stepfather, my sister Robin, and Ms. Josephine at a local restaurant to celebrate a mission completed. The last time Ms. Josephine and I were in each other's presence was August of 1969, when she gave me my first bath and wrapped me in a swaddle to prepare me for what was to come. After we were seated and our meals arrived, the moment I was waiting for began. Ms. Josephine shared her version of my earliest beginnings by substantiating portions of a story I was told many years earlier. However, her version included greater detail and was like walking backwards into time. Ms. Josephine smiled as she recounted the moments after I took my first breath. Her voice resonated deep inside me, and I hung onto every word.

At some point, Ms. Josephine said that she had not spoken a word about my birth and availability for adoption since contacting my mother and telling her of my availability. It seemed as if the more she spoke, everything was coming back to her memory as if they had just occurred. Ms. Josephine told me that she and a coworker considered adopting me after she was unsuccessful in talking my birth mother out of putting me up for adoption.

According to Ms. Josephine, she pleaded with my birth mother to keep me, and when she wouldn't budge, she suggested that she take me home to her family as it was not uncommon at the time for aunts, grandmothers, uncles, and sometimes older siblings to raise other family member's children as their own to keep families together.

Despite having already given up her firstborn to her uncle at sixteen, my birth mother placed me into adoption when she was twenty-two years old. Ms. Josephine said she tried very hard to talk some sense into my birth mother but was unsuccessful. Without holding me once and never taking the time to give me a name, three days after my birth, and before she could have been properly discharged my birth mother walked out of the hospital leaving me behind in the room we shared for a few hours.

Breakfast of Closure

The following morning after meeting my birth mother, I awoke feeling energized and refreshed. With a small amout of information and a fake name, I was able to secure my history for my children and the generations to come. I felt reborn after receiving the closure I needed, wanted, and quite frankly deserved! I thanked my mother once again for her love and understanding and discussed the strength of our bond and my appreciation of her blessings to find my biological people.

Figure 66. John having breakfast with his sister (l) Robin and his uncle(r) Eddie, Orlando, Florida, September 2019

Robin and I left my mother's home, and before separating, we met up with Uncle-Daddy for breakfast to discuss the events of the day before. There we were my youngest paternal sister and my maternal uncle laughing and enjoying each other's company filled with admiration, love, and respect. I thought, *It doesn't get any better than this!* The three of us hugged and shared pleasantries and soon parted ways. Uncle-Daddy was local and headed home to complete his schoolwork toward a terminal degree that he began after claiming his inspiration for starting the program came from a conversation he and I had when we first met. My sister set out on a three-hour drive home to prepare for work on the next day, and I drove to the airport to turn in my rental car and catch my flight. After going through airport security and getting onto the plane, I sat in my seat and looked out of the window as the plane taxied down the runway experiencing a feeling I had never felt until that day. For the first time in my life, the gaping hole in my heart that I've suffered with most of my life was filled. Finally, I was whole and could move forward in life with peace and purpose.

When I finally met my birth mother, I didn't get the warm reception that I hoped for, but I was not surprised by her indifference.

To see her just once and to talk with her face-to-face allowed me to gain an increased perspective on my purpose. I finally understood that my birth and the circumstances that surrounded it were preordained. I needed a mother, and Ada needed a son!

When Relationships Supersedes DNA

Before I could even begin to imagine having sisters, I had Vanessa L. Williams (not the actress but spelled the same) who to this day remains my very first sister. During my life, I have learned the true meaning of love cannot simply be expressed by words because love is a verb and can only be expressed through actions. Blood

Figure 67. Vanessa Williams and her son Jamal Mitchell

is thicker than water, but love is thicker than blood! As far back as I can remember, Vanessa has always been a pillar in the Williams' family. When it comes to family reunions and other events that required attention to detail and organizing large groups of people, she is the go-to person. Both of us were born in Orlando, but she was raised in upstate New York. In August 1997, Vanessa called to inform me she would be passing through Charlotte on her way to Atlanta.

She planned to start a new beginning with her then six-year-old son Jamal. When she eventually arrived with all her belongings packed into a U-Haul truck, she appeared to need a break from the long drive down the east coast.

During the late nineties, Charlotte, North Carolina, was one of the southeastern regions hidden gems. With its booming economy, clean streets, skyscrapers, and southern charm, the city was up and coming. Shortly after arriving, Vanessa asked to borrow my car to explore Charlotte before getting back on the highway to Atlanta. Without hesitation, I handed her my keys and volunteered to keep a watchful eye on Jamal.

The afternoon gave way to night, and she returned with a lease to an apartment in Charlotte after terminating her leasing agreement in Atlanta. Other than her son, no one would benefit from her decision to stay in Charlotte more than me. Vanessa's initial transition to the Queen City was a humble one. With a midsize U-Haul truck filled with her and her son's belongings, she hit the ground running. Just inside one year, with a strong work ethic and no car, she became a homeowner and bought an SUV.

When I was a bachelor, she ensured I had a home-cooked meal and was always ready to listen to issues I was experiencing at the time. In return, I volunteered to watch Jamal when she had to work late or simply needed time to herself. Our years together in Charlotte helped transform our friendship into what I can only call a brother-sister relationship.

After finding my biological sisters, I am certain that Vanessa and I are and forever will be siblings built through admiration, respect, trust, and a bond so strong once siblingship was discovered, it placed everything in prospective. As time slipped into the future and I got married and later had children, Vanessa was still there. Our bond has permeated throughout my entire family, my wife and children love her just as I do! Now that we are older, Vanessa has reciprocated my acts of kindness a hundredfold. With short notice, she has crossed several states to watch my children when my wife and I needed her help. Vanessa has become a vital part of my household. When it came time for me to chase after my biological family history, she was there to provide encouragement, love, and support. Despite us not sharing the same bloodline, Vanessa has been close to me for so long that our oldest children have now reach adulthood.

"By the power invested in me as a man who is now comfortable in his own skin, I upgrade my cousin by adoption to my sister for life!"

My Rib

In 1997, I lived in Charlotte, North Carolina, enjoying my life living as an extreme bachelor after two failed marriages and was only twenty-eight years old. I vowed to myself that I would only get married again when hell froze over, and I didn't shy away from sharing my position with anyone who'd stop long enough to listen.

During this period in my life I was a U.S. Army Recruiter and, if I must admit, a very good one. In the late nineties, an army recruiter's entire life revolved around weekly requirements that gave way to monthly quotas, which usually wasn't a concern of mine because I easily achieved my quotas. Because of my natural ability to sale intangible items, such as the army, on most

Figure 68. Rolonda Payne on her wedding day, August 21, 1999

evenings, I could leave the office earlier than my colleagues.

Before leaving, I usually performed a skit for my colleagues who had to remain in the office making cold calls to schedule appointments. During my skit, I would act as if I pulled the pin of a hand grenade with my teeth and toss the hand grenade into the center of the office, followed by me making an explosion sound. Just before actually leaving, I would turn to face my colleagues and motion my arms and hands as if I were spreading tacks on the floor to prevent them from following me out of the door. As a child, I recalled the spreading of tacks were used as a defensive measure in old kung fu movies. One particular evening while acting out my skit, my supervisor asked if he could have a word with me, and I obliged. He began by acknowledging my monthly accomplishments and requested that I ride along with him to help the team meet its monthly quota. Even though my individual quota had been met, I didn't have a problem helping the team and found myself headed out with my supervisor to canvass or, as we used to call it, conducting face-to-face prospecting. We ended up at the local mall passing out business cards and flyers in hopes of garnering an appointment that would hopefully lead to a commitment. While walking the hallways, I noticed a young woman working inside a jewelry store. I don't have an explanation for what came over me, but it was a feeling I had never felt before that moment nor have I experienced it since. My supervisor asked, "What's wrong, Payne?"

I enthusiastically responded, "I just saw my wife!"

He sarcastically replied, "Yeah, right! They're all your wives!"

My supervisor laughed at my moment of sudden revelation because he was a witness to my casual and haphazard life at the time. I then said to him, "No, man, I'm serious," as I made a bee-line toward the beautiful young woman who I knew in that moment would become my wife. I introduced myself to her, and we have been together ever since.

On August 21, 1999, Rolonda L. Allen and I were married, and our union produced three wonderful children that include John III, Sean, and Jocelyn.

Figure 69. The Payne Family at the graduation of their first born: (l to r top row) Dr. Rolonda L. Payne, John I. Payne III, John I. Payne, Jr.; (l to r bottom row) Jocelyn M. Payne, and Sean A. Payne, 2019.

As a young man raised in church, I heard about scripture speaking to man's need for a companion and God using one of Adam's ribs to form Eve. Although I heard this many times, I didn't have a literal understanding until several years after my wife and I were married. By no means will I tell anyone or paint a picture of a perfect marriage, but through prayer and perseverance and a relationship deeply immersed in friendship, we have established a bond that is stronger than the storms the world has thrown at us. When I met the family of my then girlfriend for the first time, I observed the respect she had for her father.

As the years began to add up, her unconditional love for me began to shine through. Because of my obligation to my army career, my wife was the lynchpin that held our family together until I was able to realign my priorities. My wife has supported me above and beyond what my expectations could ever conceive.

Because of my two failed marriages, I thought it best to disclose to my then fiancée that I was adopted. As part of our premarital arrangements, we agreed to get counseling where my adoptive status was discussed because I wanted to give our marriage the best chance possible.

On several occasions, I found myself deeply submerged in a black hole of pity because of my lack of understanding of how challenging the deficiency of physical genetic mirroring impacted me, both growing up and in my adult life, but my wife was always there to provide me with encouragement. When I decided to submit my DNA for the purpose of finding my bloodline, my wife was by my side. When I felt as though I couldn't go on or take another step toward success in any challenge or undertaken, my wife was there to provide her unique special blend of love and uplift. When my DNA began to yield blood relatives and siblings, not once did she complain.

My wife's love for me made room for others because she cares so much about my happiness and well-being. I am forever indebted to her for her love, loyalty, and friendship!

The Pen Is Mightier Than the Sword

January 8, 2020, began with a feeling of heaviness in my chest because of the sadness I felt for Uncle-Daddy, as it was only the night before that I received word his firstborn child, Andrew Vandale Peterson, had passed away. I hadn't met my first cousin, but I did remember the admiration his siblings showed whenever his name was mentioned.

After gathering the details about his memorial service, I contacted Anthony to ask him about his travel plans to pay final respects to our cousin. We agreed that both of us wanted to attend the memorial service, but during the call, we did not finalize our modes of transportation.

After consulting with my wife, I decided that I would drive to Orlando, and take my two youngest children along with me. I thought it would be a great opportunity for them to spend time with their grandmother, Ada. During a follow-up call with Anthony, we decided he would drive from New York to my home in Maryland and then ride with me and my children to Orlando.

Although not a pleasure trip, I was optimistic about the positive things that could be accomplished by visiting Orlando, including having an even greater opportunity to build the bond between my oldest maternal brother and me; my two youngest children getting the opportunity to spend time with their grandmother; being able to fellowship with my maternal family members; and most importantly, supporting my Uncle-Daddy who would be eulogizing his firstborn child. Anthony arrived at my home on the Thursday before the memorial service was to be held.

Friday morning, Anthony, my children, and I headed for I-95, my favorite interstate because it takes me to all the places I like to be. In fact, I have never turned down a trip to Florida and more than likely never will. When we reached South Carolina, I made a detour in Columbia to check on my families first home turned rental property. We also used the detour as a break from the monotony of a long drive and to stretch our legs for a few minutes. While in Columbia, I was able to schedule an appointment with my old barber before getting back on the interstate. We finally arrived in Orlando late Friday night, and I dropped Anthony off at a cousin's apartment, and my children and I continued to my parents' home.

In keeping with the facts surrounding my life—being adopted and finding my biological family—I couldn't help but think about my biological mother. She gave birth to three sons and doesn't have a decent relationship with either one of us. I thought about having to drop off Anthony, her eldest son and my brother, at a cousin's apartment instead of our biological mother's house. Anthony wasn't welcome in the house of our birth mother, not even for a good-night's sleep after a long road trip to memorialize our first cousin, and our birth mothers' nephew.

On Saturday, January 25, 2020, my children and I awoke in a comfortable and familiar place; the home of the person I believe is the greatest mother in the world! The first call I received that morning was from Anthony. He called to let me know that I didn't have to pick him up because he was going to catch a ride to the memorial service with Kim, our cousin. Afterward, I got myself together for the drive to the church, which was only a short distance from my childhood home. Due to my disdain for tardiness, I found myself in the familiar situation of having lots of time on my hands before the scheduled time for the family to assemble in the church parking lot.

I decided to drive to the other side of town for a cup of coffee to kill time and reflect on the gravity of losing a loved one and what it meant to the many people that knew and loved Andrew.

After returning to the church, I met the family in the parking lot where we assembled for our single file entrance into the church. Once inside, I sat and listened to Andrew's siblings and children share emotional verbal vignettes about his life and legacy. Soon thereafter, Uncle-Daddy stood behind the podium centered on the pulpit and delivered nothing short of a eulogy created from pure genius. During the eulogy, I thought what an undertaking it must be for him to lose a son and, moreover, to exhibit such courage and resolve eulogizing him.

Figure 70. Rev. Dr. Eddie L. Harris, eulogizing his firstborn Andrew V. Peterson, January 25, 2020, Orlando, Florida

The memorial service ended, and after taking a few pictures with my maternal family members, Anthony and I got into my truck and followed Uncle-Daddy to the repast. After a short while of mingling with family, Uncle-Daddy and I agreed to make our final rounds before we departed the repast to share some uncle-nephew time, as my stay in Orlando was understandably short. Before leaving the repast, Uncle-Daddy's youngest son, Dallis, recommended one of my uncle's favorite restaurants. I mentioned the restaurant to Uncle-Daddy, and he said, "Oh yeah, I like that place," so we agreed to go there.

He followed me to my mother's house and parked his car out front so that we could ride together.

Every moment of my journey of discovery has become moments of learning. I believe these learning moments were available long before I began my quest to find my bloodline. However, people can see only when their eyes become open, and now I pay much closer attention to the many gifts that I am being rewarded. For example, my biological uncle has met my mother, who is not his sister, and they both accept and respect each other. My biological uncle is accepted in my mother's home, but I am not welcome in the home of my biological mother.

Yet Uncle-Daddy can park his car on my mother's property without a worry. Uncle-Daddy jumped into my truck, and we headed for an evening of fellowship and somewhere we could take our minds off the events of the day if only for a short while. Not long after leaving my mother's house, we arrived at the restaurant and I parked the truck. We headed inside for what I knew would be a refreshing moment between us. I opened the door to allow him to enter first, as we walked toward the waitress standing behind a small wooden podium to request seating.

I observed several ladies of the Alpha Kappa Alpha Sorority, Incorporated sitting near the front of the restaurant enjoying the camaraderie afforded them as sorority sisters.

Uncle-Daddy and I are proud members of Omega Psi Phi Fraternity, Incorporated, so I found it appropriate to tell him about the AKA's. "Table for two," I said after reaching the podium.

And the woman standing there said, "Follow me please."

We followed her through the restaurant to our table, and a waiter approached us to take our drink requests. I ordered a "Tiger Woods," which is my comedic spin on the popular drink Arnold Palmer. The Arnold Palmer consists of one-part lemonade and one-part sweet tea.

I jokingly call it a Tiger Woods because I prefer my Arnold Palmer's a little heavy on the sweet tea side. There we sat, having thought-provoking conversation that I always find mentally stimulating when I'm with Uncle-Daddy. It made me feel good to help shift his mind away, if only for a short time, from the pressure I knew he must have felt after losing and eulogizing his eldest son. Although I wasn't hungry, I ordered fish and grits, and Uncle-Daddy followed suit.

After sitting together and barely eating, we gave in, and both requested carryout containers, paid the bill, and then headed for the door.

While walking toward the door, I noticed the AKA's were no longer sitting near the front of the restaurant and it was nearly vacant due to their departure.

We exited the restaurant and headed in the direction of the parking lot when we heard a voice yell, "Eddie Harris!" Both of us turned to look behind us in the direction where the voice came from. I noticed two ladies sitting on a bench at the front right of the restaurant's entrance. After recognizing an old friend, Uncle-Daddy responded, "Hey, girl, how are you doing?" I continued walking to my truck, barely breaking my stride. I placed my carryout on the back seat, started the engine, and closed the driver's door.

I called my wife to ask about her day and to share information about mine. I also called my mother to check on her and the kids, and to ask if she wanted me to pick anything up on my way home. After completing my calls, I directed my attention back to Uncle-Daddy, observing his every move through my rearview mirror. I don't know the intricate details of their conversation, but whatever the topic, it lasted at least twenty-five minutes before he made his way back to the truck, only to drop off his things, grab his business cards, and to ask me to get out of the truck to meet the two ladies sitting on the bench waiting on his return.

Uncle-Daddy and I have had conversations on many occasions about my desire to join the fight against unfair adoption laws and practices in the state of Florida. As he was placing his things in the truck and grabbing his business cards, he told me that one of the ladies was a judge and she might know the judge who answered my petition to open my once closed and sealed adoption case. I turned the truck off and walked back to the front of the restaurant with Uncle-Daddy to meet the last two AKA's still there, one of them being a friend of my uncle. "Ladies, I would like to introduce you to my nephew-son. His name is John Payne." I have lived on this planet for fifty years, and until my uncle and I established our relationship, I have never heard anyone introduced with a title like the one Uncle-Daddy has given me. My introduction alone could not be ignored and required explanation. Uncle-Daddy told the ladies, "I have to tell you a story about my nephew," and then he began to share the beginnings of our relationship with them. I briefly interrupted him and suggested that I take a seat. I know our story has many nuances that cannot be easily explained, and I also knew it may take a while. I sat down between the pair of strangers on the bench that I had walked by twice that evening. Uncle-Daddy delved deeper and deeper into the story about our connection and, at one point, turned to me and said,

"Okay, nephew-son, you take over from here," as if he just completed his leg of a 4x100-meter relay and was passing the baton to me.

I began my leg of the story by describing a letter I wrote that subsequently transformed into a petition to the Circuit Court of the Ninth Judicial Circuit of Orange County, Florida. I rambled on about how my letter ended up in the hands of a judge who is a member of Alpha Kappa Alpha Sorority, Incorporated.

The two strangers listened intensely and seemingly held onto my every word. At one point, I turned to the lady sitting to my right and continued telling my story from the point when the judge assigned a lawyer to assist me in my quest to reopen my closed and sealed adoption case. When I mentioned "assigning a lawyer," the lady to my right spoke aloud

Figure 71. John meets Judge Tanya Davis-Wilson, January 25, 2020

the name of the lawyer who was assigned to my case. Beginning to feel a sense of amazement, I asked her a few rhetorical questions in the form of statements for confirmation of the unbelievable feelings I was experiencing. I asked, "You are an AKA? You are a judge?"

I can't remember if she answered my questions or not, but I will never forget her placing both hands over her mouth, as tears began to roll down her face. Feeling emotional too, I asked her, "What is your name?"

With extreme humility, she replied, "Tanya Wilson!" At that very moment, all four of us were fully aware of the overwhelming improbability of what was taking place. When she said her name, it was as if a hand grenade was detonated in the center of where the three of us were sitting. Just as everything became clear to all of us, simultaneously, the glaring truth caused us to jump to our feet and walk away in four different directions with disbelief about God's explosive power being revealed before our very eyes.

To put this into context, I drove 852 miles in just over twelve hours to attend the memorial service of a cousin who I unfortunately never had the pleasure of meeting and dined at a recommended restaurant I've never heard of before that day. According to usapopulation.org, in 2019, there was 290,000 people living in Orlando, and like a needle in a haystack, God allowed me to meet the Honorable Judge Tanya Davis-Wilson.

Figure 72. The Honorable Judge Tonya Davis-Wilson

Judge Davis-Wilson is the very person who on February 5, 2018, signed an order that opened my closed and sealed adoption records that were buried deep in the long-forgotten history of adoptions in the state of Florida. Her signature alone created the path to unlocking my lost but not forgotten linage and allowed me access to my birthright, knowing where I came from and from whom.

"The pen is mightier than the sword!"

About the Author

John I Payne Jr. was born in Orlando, Florida on August 9, 1969. Adopted at birth, he went on to graduate from Jones High School before enlisting into the US Army. While in the Army John achieved a Bachelors of Science degree and a Masters in Business Administration before retiring from the military with 20 years of honorable service. He is a husband of more than 20 years and a father of three children.

John is a proud member of Omega Psi Phi Fraternity, Inc., and also a member of the American Adoption Congress (ACC) which is an International organization devoted to family connections. He is also a strong advocate for the adoptees "Right to Know"! The Right to Know, is the granting of all adoptees access to their heritage regardless of the circumstances leading up to our being placed into adoption.

CPSIA information can be obtained
at www.ICGtesting.com
Printed in the USA
BVHW022045220321
603191BV00016B/431

9 781648 015847